Bullied: Dying to Fit In was nominated and received the
Advocacy/Social Justice Award for the 2019
In the Margins Book Award
School Library Journal

This is every bullied person's story.
Will you listen?

Metamorphosis is to evolve from one creature, like a caterpillar, into another, a butterfly.

Bullied.

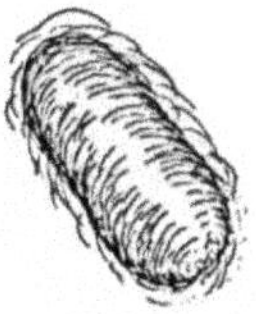

Healing.

Free.

Being bullied can make you feel like a bug that can get squashed at any moment. But, once you realize by transforming yourself and becoming who you really are, you can develop into the butterfly that takes wing and is set free from the pain.

Bullied

Dying to Fit In

Normandy D. Piccolo

NBI
Normandy's Bright Ideas

Bullied Dying to Fit In
Printed in the United States of America

ISBN: 978-0-9979349-4-6

An educational read for schools, counselors and children being bullied to better learn about bullying and its long-term effects.

For additional information about *Bullied Dying to Fit In,* please visit www. normandydpiccolo.com

contents

Bullied Dying to Fit In is for the bullied and the bully. It reveals the raw feelings and emotions a person might experience because of bullying. It also shows a strong correlation between bullying and mental health issues, like depression.

Did you know a bullied person's feelings and emotions can overwhelm them to the point of considering suicide to stop the pain?

Stories about kids committing suicide because of bullying make daily headlines around the globe and yet, the number of deaths because of bullying continue to rise and the ages are getting younger. Why? Because the emotional/mental fallout from being bullied has not been recognized, nor understood well enough.

Too much effort is spent on promoting T shirts, bracelets and witty little sayings against bullying. While those things help bring awareness to the issue of bullying and certain mental health issues amplified or formed due to bullying, they do not offer solutions.

Keeping things surface and *"not going there"* because the topic of depression, self-harm and suicide is too unpleasant, is getting us nowhere. We need to deal with this unpleasant topic head-on and acknowledge the gritty, raw side of bullying and intensified mental health issues either amplified or formed because of it.

Bullied Dying to Fit In talks to you. Not at you. It helps one to understand the reality of what can happen if bullying goes too far, before transitioning into positive reinforcement, guidance and wisdom.

After reading this book, a person being bullied will hopefully understand why they are being bullied, how to stop being a victim of bullying and develop a realistic, but, still positive outlook on their life.

warning: The desire to quit life is expressed in parts of the book because that is the truth. Committing suicide is strongly discouraged as a solution to fixing bullying and/or mental health issues. If you or anyone you know are struggling with any of those issues, please seek help at a support or crisis center in your area or online through local and national organizations.

SUICIDE IS NEVER THE ANSWER.

sadness

bad days 95%
good days 5%

how should i end it and if i did would you care?

How should I end it and if I did, would you care?
I could cut my veins open and let blood ooze everywhere.

How should I end it and if I did, would you run?
I could wrap my lips around the barrel and pull the trigger of a gun.

How should I end it and if I did, would you feel a sharp pang?
I could noose a belt around my neck, jump off a chair and hang.

How should I end it and if I did, would you let out a shrill?
I could get a glass of water and down a bottle of sleeping pills.
Why should I end it? It's because of your hate.
You say hurtful things, you spit on my lunch plate.

You say you're just kidding, but that's not the truth.
Want to know how I know?
I'll tear open my chest and show you the proof.

My heart is riddled with pain, hurt and misery.
Why should I end it?
It's because you won't let me be.

Maybe I'll fight back...maybe, we'll see.
But, if I should end it just know this one thing.
I ended it because of you, you cruel, heartless, mean thing.

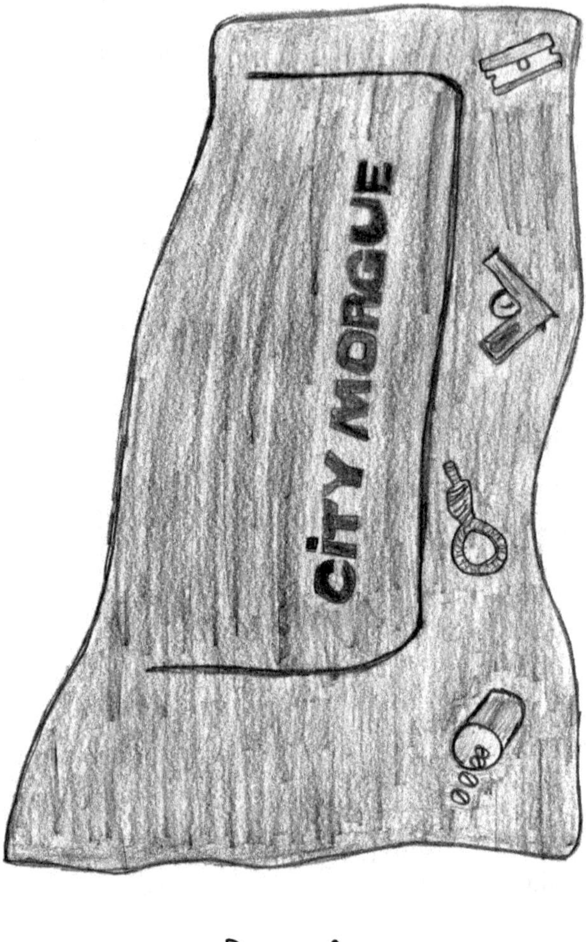

Dying to fit in
Dying to be someone's friend
Died because the bullying never came to an end.

the kid whose name nobody knew

OBITUARY NOTICE

✝

The Kid Whose Name Nobody Knew, 14, died January 20, from a self-inflicted injury due to relentless bullying.

The Kid was talented, intelligent, caring, giving, thoughtful, and a hard worker. But, due to the ignorant cruelty of fellow classmates, only the Kid's family knew of those things.

The Kid was born surrounded by love and died alone, feeling rejected, depressed, hurt and confused.

The Kid will be best remembered as the one who got pelted in the school halls with water bottles, gossiped about on social media, punched, kicked, spat upon and excluded from social events.

The Kid lived what's deemed the "best years", as the "worst years". The Kid never understood why nobody would be a friend. The Kid tried to be a friend to everyone.

The Kid is survived by two grieving parents who will spend the rest of their days brokenhearted, trying to understand why their child chose suicide as the answer to being bullied.

In lieu of flowers please contribute to the Kid's memory by not being a bully.

beware of the closet

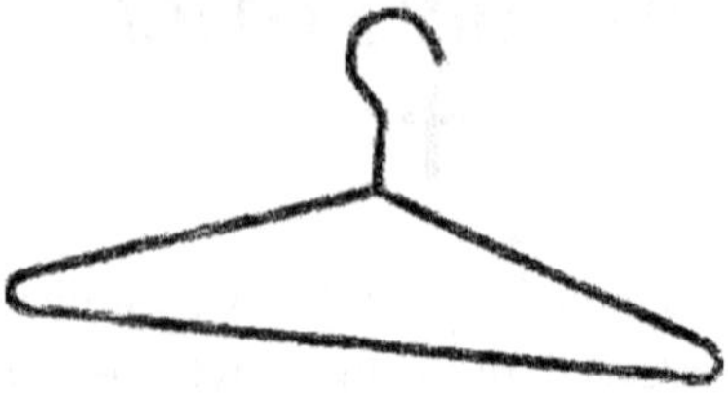

Beware of the closet
It is where hurtful secrets hide
Beware of the closet
Venture inside and you might die

Beware of the closet
A roped serpent dangles above from a wire shelf
Beware of the closet
Peace may not thrive while hanging yourself

Beware of the closet
Rumors and lies are meant to deceive
Beware of the closet
Stop! Don't hand your life over to a lying thief

But, I want to go into the closet
Make a noose, let the pain end
I want to go into the closet
For I am nobody's friend

I want to go into the closet
I hate the way I feel
So, what if I hang myself?
It's not that big of a deal

I want to go into the closet
Silence the repetitious voices inside my head
I want to go into the closet
Kids at school say they wish I were dead

I want to go into the closet
Nobody wants me around anyway
I want to go into the closet
I want the world to stay away

The closet represents darkness
It's where truth, half-truths and skeletons reside
But, if I choose to stay out of the closet
Then, I won't, I don't have to die

One step in
Another step back out
I pull on my hair
I scream, and I shout

F**k you!
I hate you!

You fail me again and again
Why do I have to make this choice?
Why did you push me to the end?

No! No! No!
I scream then slam the closet door shut
I drop down to the floor
And tell the pain, *"Shut up!"*

I then let out a wailing cry
God, please show me how to survive
Life, come on, stop failing me
Please, help me, I need to revive

I mean, why should I give up?
Why should I let them beat me?
If I go into the closet and hang myself
I'll be labeled a sell-out, a wimp or a wussy

Church once taught me that suicide's a sin
So, if I quit and go into the closet
I lose
They win

No! No! No!
I won't give up that quick
I won't let them get the better of me
I'm no longer absorbing their sh**

I am staying out of the closet
At least, now, for me
I am not going to exhale
No! Instead, I am going to breathe!

I never knew a text
That became a private sext
Would be sent out to everyone
by a bitter, spiteful Ex

Hester Prynne always felt hexed
A giant red letter placed upon her chest
But, that was not my case
I did not lust after another or give chase

So, why is an A now on my chest?
What? Because I sent my then boyfriend a sext?
Seriously? That makes me a slut?
I feel like I've been punched in the gut

I wish I could take it back
I wish I could take it back
I only wish

If I had known my bitter Ex
Would show the world the private sext
I never would have sent it
And now, it's too late to relent it

But, I do know this one thing
I will never, ever send another sext
I will not dare trust, nor flex

For if you should ask me for a sext
My reply to you will simply be, NEXT!

Punch me
Slap me
Say mean things about me
Guess what? I feel
How can you not believe my pain isn't real?

I am broken.

Meet my friend
Who goes by the name of unbelievable pain
It resides deep inside my heart
And courses through my veins
Thanks to your unbelievable pain
Life is no longer fun
Then, more vicious verbal vomit spews forth
And everything comes undone
That is when it ventures outside
By rolling down my cheeks
Encased inside many salty tears
The only way it speaks.

I am not a slut
You said that you cared
I believed that you liked me
Not because of a frat boy dare

I let you take pictures
You promised not to share
But, you betrayed me you liar
And now, the pictures are everywhere

You made me popular
But, not in the right way
Girls want to kick my ass
Boys look to get laid

I hate you! I hate you! I hate you!
How could you do me wrong?
I would never have hurt you
I had loved you for so long

The pain that you caused me
Can never be erased
Nor can the pictures,
Now the world knows my face.

Pump me
Hump me
Then treat me like trash
Popular I've become
Voted the school's favorite piece of ass

With boys in the dark
I'm pretty, I'm the bell
However, by myself
I'm ashamed, I'm in hell

If, I don't do what they ask
I won't be desired, I won't be wanted
Little did I know in the end
I'd be rejected and brutally taunted

A thousand douches, a million showers
Won't ever make me feel clean
I've gone from being popular
To a, "*She'll do it with anyone*" sleaze queen

Comments written on social media walls
Vulgar words shouted in the halls
"For a good time, call"
Scribbled inside a bathroom stall

I don't care
Say what you will
Your words can't hurt me
Remember, I'm so popular, I'm chill

But, that's the problem
The reality is, I do
I can try to front until I graduate
But, down inside it's the painful truth

Sleeping around to be popular
Is not all it's cracked up to be
I wish I could go back on it all
Erase it or undue everything

But, I felt insecure
And wanted to fit in
Like the other girls
I was lonely, in need of a friend

I'll never understand
Why it's okay that some girls can
While other girls who do the same
Get slut-shamed, again and again.

A release from the pain
The razor blade exposes my sins
Penetrating, slicing, it rips apart my skin

I don't want to die
I just want some peace
With each cut I make
I begin to feel some relief.

My emotional wounds run deeper than the cuts on my flesh.

This cut is for wanting to belong and not.
This cut is for life not getting better even when I try.
This cut is for getting beat up when I speak up.

This cut is for the rumors spread about me.
This cut is for the shame I now feel about myself.
This cut is for the sorrow I'm drowning in.

This cut is for the rejection.
This cut is for feeling isolated.

This cut is for making me hate myself.
This cut is for feeling so helpless, weak and pathetic.
This cut is to awaken the numbness.

This cut is to feel something. I feel nothing anymore.
This cut is for being a loser. A nothing. A nobody.
This cut is for being empty inside.

This cut is for being bullied.

I'm running out of places to cut.

Please bring it to an end.

I don't think I can take much more!

I once was a seedling
planted into the ground
I grew big, I was strong
until they cut me down

I was pressed and pressured
and watered down
Before being placed in a factory where
others like me abound

Scissors and razor blades
They brought me relief
Tormented inside
I found a release

I'm but a paper doll
Fragile and weak
Rough around the edges
Too pathetic to speak

A paper cut I can give you
Compared to what you gave me
The pain of rejecting myself
Pain so strong, I can hardly breathe.

Playing *'Rock - Paper – Scissors'* with a bully.
Rock I throw at you.
Scissors I cut with to relieve the pain you've caused.
Paper I write my final goodbyes'.

The cuts continue to appear
Though I keep hoping to disappear

From my body, the blood runs down
But, I hear not a single sound

Just the faint whimpers of my soul as it cries
Why? Why? Why? Oh, why?

Drip, by drip, by drip
On their radar of destruction,
I am nothing to them but a blip.

My family thinks I'm strong
A bully sees me as weak
A smile for Mom and Dad
Secret slaps across my cheek

I wish I could tell my parents
So, they might help it stop
But, if I open my mouth and speak
The bully finds out, I'll get popped

So, I front for Mom and Dad
Weep silent tears into my sleeve
Reaping kicks, hits and punches
In private, I continuously grieve.

Overwhelmed
Under-loved
Beaten badly
Constantly shoved
Bruises hurt
Tears trickle down
Confusion sets in
So much hurt I could drown.

I feel sad.
I feel depressed.
I feel anxious.
I feel sick.
I feel unwanted.
I feel left out.
I feel lonely.
I feel so tired.
I feel like giving up.
I feel I can't take another day.
I feel lots of other things, too.
But, I don't feel loved or that I'll be missed.

Wish I could say
But bad feelings won't go away
I want so much to stray
But, something keeps making me stay

I really want to live
I have so much to give
But, no one seems to want me
Everyone in school endlessly taunts me

I cup my hands over my ears
Sing loudly so I can't hear
But, the hateful words manage to seep in
I fight back the tears, but the crying begins

Alone under the stairs
No one seems to care
I hold my knees close to my chest
I feel as if I'm failing life's test

Dork, Jerk, Geek, Loser, Ass
The bell just rang, now I'm late for class

I don't want to come out for fear of being hit
Why am I always picked on?
Why does the world think I'm shit?

See me with a bullet in my head?
See me with the noose wrapped around my neck?
See me swallow an entire bottle of pills?
See me slash my wrists until the blood spills?

Watch me get lowered into the ground
The dirt covers me over
You say no words, make no sound

You won't shed one tear
No water for my flowers to grow
Only emit cheers of joy and say,
"Another dork dead. That's how it goes."

I will be, but a memory is what I've been told
My locker will be emptied, my clothes will be sold

No one will miss me, or so they type
Sure, my death will be news, until the next hype

Stupid, dumb, ugly, fat, loser, lame
You should die they said, imagine the fame

Newspapers, Television, Facebook, Twitter
Problem is, my parents said they didn't raise no quitter

Miss me, don't miss me, I suppose that's your choice
Will your heart even break?
Will your eyes become moist?

Do it
Don't do it
Not sure which one will win
Die before it's time
Heard that's a big sin

Stupid, dumb, ugly, fat, loser, lame
How I wish I could start over
How I hate this hurtful game.

Would you miss me if I went away?
Would you pause for a moment?
Beg me not to die, not to decay?

Is there someone, anyone, willing to say,
"Please, stay."
Nothing but silence.
Apparently, not today.

I never wanted to cry because I was bullied.
I never wanted to cry for being called hurtful names.
I never wanted to cry for being beat up for no reason.
I never wanted to cry for rumors spread about me.
I never wanted to cry because of those things.
But, I cry now all the time.

Sometimes I just need a hug and to be told, *"Everything is going to be all right"*, even if it might never be.

So young.
So beautiful.
So tragic.
Now gone.
Will you even miss me?

I need love. Not hate.

No Slut Am I
I will always deny
The vicious rumors you
continually spread
To silence your voice
I shall have to be dead
To get your hateful words
Flushed out of my head.

No one cares.

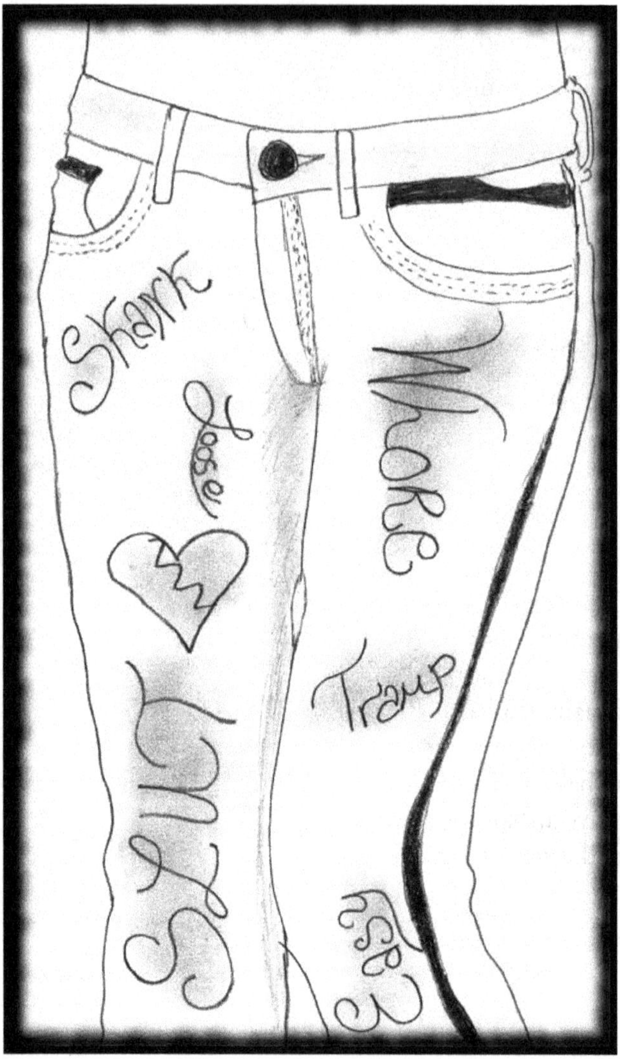
Skank
Loose
Whore
Tramp
Slut

Nobody cares.
They stare.
Or, they glare.
Speak a kind word to me?
Pah! They would never dare.

I am a light.
I want to shine.
But I can't.
They won't let me.

Why don't I fit in?
Why won't they let me fit in?
I don't understand.

Sorry I'm not perfect like you.

So, I'm short
So, I'm a little fat
So, my hair's curly
Instead of being flat
I like myself.

So, I love to smile
So, I sometimes cry
So, I don't give up
So, I give it another try.
I like myself.

Then I met you.

Now, my feelings hurt
Now, you make me sad
Now, I smile no more
Now, I always feel sad
I hate myself.

I hate that I am short
I hate that I am fat
I hate my curly hair
I wish it would go flat
I hate myself.

I no longer smile
All I do is cry
No matter what I say or do
My life is full of sighs
I really hate myself.

What did I do wrong?
Why do I even give a damn?
I am so tired of trying to prove myself to you
Why can't you just accept me the way that I am?

While I loathe you, just know, I hate myself even more.

If you prick me
I bleed just the same
You call me a slut
But, that is not my name

If you hit me
I shed tears
But, do you?
The pain that I feel
I hope someday you feel, too

Please, please ignore me
Disappear and go away
Never bother me again
That's all I must say.

Shut up! Shut up! Just go away!
Social media sites are where you go to say
Hurtful, hateful, cruel remarks you proudly speak
Singling me out because you assume I am weak

But, you are the one who is weak
For you type crap, but never speak
I dare you to say those words to my face
To come and invade my personal space

You can't, I suppose.
I'm not surprised, it figures.
You're just a coward behind the keyboard
Typing lies with a click and a snicker

You are pathetic!

I left something for you at your front door last night.
My shoes.

I wonder if you will dare to wear them.
To step into the hell, you have created for me.

I wish you would put my shoes on your feet.
I wish you would feel the pain you have caused me.

I want you to feel each step taken as if it were going to be your last. Because, that is how I feel every single day.

Dammit!

I just want you to feel what I feel.
If you did, maybe you would stop bullying me. But, I doubt it.

You can keep my shoes as a reminder. To never forget what you did, even though you will probably forget about me.

will you?

Will you punch me when no one is around?

Will you always call me hurtful names?

Will you line up chairs at the head of the room and mock my funeral when I come into class?

Will you write nasty limericks about me on the bathroom wall and proudly sign your name?

Will you shove me?

Will you throw water bottles at me and get everyone else to do the same as I am walking down the halls at school?

Will you get someone to pretend to like me, so I will share my innermost thoughts, then use what you learned about me against me?

Will you nominate me for Class President and get my hopes up to win, only to have the whole school laugh at me?

Will you post endless lies about me on the internet?

Will you harass me to the point where I don't want to leave my house anymore?

Will you invite me to a party and then, when I show up, pretend you never invited me?

Will you do those things?
Will you?

Your answer is YES, you will. Because you have already done those things to me.

Since you are so willing I would like to know...

Will you help me drape the belt up in the closet?

Will you form a strong noose to break my neck?

Will you kick the chair out from underneath me?

Will you hold my feet, so they don't wildly kick about while I'm asphyxiating to death?

Will you even try and stop me from ending my life?

Your answer is NO, you will not. Because you willfully drove me to this decision.

Will you wait around while my organs shut down?
That is, assuming my neck doesn't snap right away.

Will you still wait anyway, as I linger for a while, breathing very, very shallow breaths. This could take a while. Hope you brought something to read.

Will you watch my face twist and contort?

Will you take pictures and post them?

Will you then brag and say, *"Look What I Made Happen."* You must be so proud of yourself.

Will you cut me down or leave me hanging alone in the closet?

Will you leave the closet light on or leave me swinging ever so slightly, back and forth in the dark?

I can't help but wonder.

Will you clean me up after I have crapped and pissed my pants? You know that happens during asphyxiation, right?

Will you clean up the mess I made?

Will you redress me?

When my parents ask you, *"Why did this happen?"*

Will you tell them the truth?

Will you tell my parents about all the mean things you said and did to me?

Will you tell my parents how sorry you are for doing and saying mean, hateful things to me?

Will you even mean it?

I doubt it.

Will you help my parents plan my funeral?

Will you help my parents pick out a coffin?

Will you help my parents pick out an outfit for me to be buried in?

Will you place a flower, or an apology note on my coffin?

Will you say something nice about me at my funeral?

Will your words be full of regret for the way you treated me while I was alive, or will you spew more hate?

Will you even comprehend the money my parents had saved for my college fund is now paying for my funeral?

Will you even care that instead of a graduate certificate, I get a death certificate now, instead?

Will you help my parents pack up my room and donate some of my stuff while storing the rest?

Will you keep in touch with my parents? See how they are doing as time marches onward?

If your answer is, *"No"*, then leave me the hell alone!

Rumors. Lies. Punches. Slaps.
I am as numb on the inside as I am on the outside.

Watch what you post
Watch what you say
The rumors you type won't ever go away

You can try to delete them, but they spread very fast
Be careful speaking untruths about someone's past

The pain you cause will never go away
So, think before you act
It's all I must say.

Could have been something.
Should have been something.
Might have been something.
Schoolmates think I am nothing.
Because of your lies.
Now, I think I am nothing, too.

I am damaged by your cruel words.
I am ravaged by your hateful friends.
I am savaged by your punches and kicks.
I am bloody.
I am wounded.
I am done.

I am plastic wrap, invisible until you spy me.
Then, I become wax paper.
Torn apart easily with your words not watered down.
You think yourself to be tinfoil.
Tough and durable.
But, what do I know
I am only plastic wrap.
Invisible.

I am so tired
I cannot sleep

Eyes open
Eyes closed

Matters not I still weep

I try to be like the other sheep
But I am cast aside and called weak

How I long to drift off,
drift off,
drift off,
And sleep

I am so tired
So tired of being called pathetic
Of being called weak

Inner strength why won't you arrive?

Until you do, I shall sit alone in my closet and weep.

I hope, one day the word BULLY disappears from the dictionary!

Monday, I got beat up.
Tuesday, more rumors were spread about me.
Wednesday, I got beat up again.
Thursday, even more rumors were spread.
Friday, I went completely numb.
Saturday, I cried in bed all day.
Sunday, I wanted to be dead.
Monday, the cycle repeats.

I am so tired of failing at life.

I am lonely.
I am heartbroken.
I hate going to school.
I love my teachers.
I hate my bully.
I want to stay home.
I never want to leave my room.
I just want to be left alone.
Why can't the world just leave me alone?

I once was a nobody
Until you made me somebody
A person who's hated by everybody

At school, I get treated like an antibody
I live inside a torn and bruised up body
Because my life you chose to disembody

I am constantly tormented soul and body
I wish I could have never been somebody
Other than that, whom I used to be, nobody.

My existence feels like one meant for you to destroy.
How I wish I did not exist right now.
How I despise your evil ploys!

A punch to my stomach.
A punch to my head.
Why prolong the misery?
I know you wish me dead.

Mean words hurt.
Cruel words cause death.
Overwhelmed by hateful blurts.
I want to take my last breath.

I stare into the bathroom mirror.
I admire zero things about myself.
I write hateful words over my reflection.
Letter by letter they effortlessly appear.
Each word, reaffirming my feelings about myself.
I spit at my reflection and scream out loud,

"Ugly! Loser! Pathetic! Nobody! Worthless! Disgusting!"

I then punch my reflection.
My hand does bleed.
My hand surely hurts.
But, if you compared that pain to that of my shattered heart – no contest. My heart hurts more.
I hate the one who I see looking back at me, more than the one who has now made me see myself this way.

I care what you think of me
I wish I knew why
Continually seeking your approval
Again, and again I try.

Why do I even bother?
What makes you so great?
You are nasty, cold and cruel.
So bitter and full of hate.

I am not okay. I may never be.

Die stupid loser.
Why are you even here?
Nobody wants to date you.
Nobody wants to be your friend.
You may as well close your eyes.
You may as well be dead.

I thought you should know, not that you care. But, what cruel things you said will hurt me forever.

You do not know me. So, shut up!

I really want to say goodbye.
I really don't want to give it another try.
Listen close.
Hear my final sigh.

Screw you once for writing mean crap on my locker.
Screw me once for not erasing it.

Screw you twice for spreading rumors about me.
Screw me twice for not telling everyone you are a liar.

Screw you three times for beating me up.
Screw me three times for taking your abuse.

Screw you four times for creating fake social media accounts in my name.
Screw me four times for not getting those accounts shut down.

Screw you five times for getting others to bully me.
Screw me five times for not reporting you.

Screw you six times for being a bully.
Screw me six times for being a victim.

SCREW YOU X infinity!!!!

Congratulations. You broke me.

A frown cannot be turned upside down, if one keeps getting beaten down.

When you call me a mean name, I feel worthless.
When you punch me in the face, I feel worthless.

When you steal my stuff, I feel worthless.

When you spread lies about me, I feel worthless.

When you bring up past mistakes I made, I feel worthless.

I wish you could understand how worthless your words and actions make me feel.

I try and feel worthy.
But you steal my joy away.
And I feel worthless, again.

I wish I was strong enough to resist your hate.
To realize you are the one who is worthless.
But I can't.
I'm too beat down.

It's raining, it's storming
Why's my life so boring?

Because…

I had some friends
But, that's come to an end
Thanks to a selfish bully.

My name is not slut.
My name is not skank.
My name is not whore.
My name is not tramp.
My name is not loser.
My name is not fat pig.
My name is not idiot.
My name is not stupid.
Do you even know my name?

My pages,
please stop stalking.
Your rumors,
please stop talking.

Smiles can be faked, you know.

Hours.
Minutes.
Seconds.
Mornings.
Afternoons.
Nights.
Days.
Weeks.
Months.
Years.
Time is no longer a friend of mine.

I don't know you.
You think you know me.
Do me a favor, huh?
Leave me be.

I am not as strong as I pretend to be.

Dejected...Subjected...Objected...and
EMO
REJECTED
LONER
FREAK
WEIRDO
STRANGE
Injection Of Your Painful Neglection
Unprotected From Your Subjected Physical Objections
Quit The Conject and Eject From My Life!

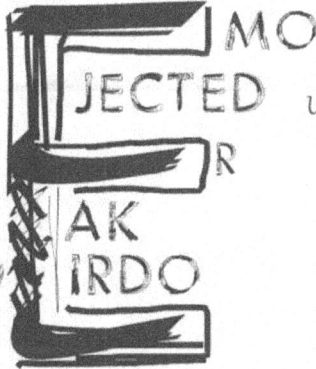

All Alone In A Tree
I'm A Sad Bird Who Sings
How I Wish I Were You
How I Wish You Were Me…
Bullying Is Crap!

If I change the shape or color of my eyes, will you see me differently?

If I shave my nose down, will you stop calling me names?
If I get my ears pinned back, will your mean words finally get blocked out?

If I grow my hair out, cut it short, change the color, straighten it, curl it, will your criticism cease?

If I pump my lips up or thin my lips down, will you stop running your lips about mine?

Nip, Tuck, Cut, Suck
My looks have now changed
And, yet, your hate remains.

My head hurts because you hit it with your fist.

My arm hurts because you twisted it behind my back.

My stomach hurts because you punched it with your other fist.

My back hurts because you kicked it with your foot.

My cheek stings because you slapped it with your hand.
My heart hurts because you spoke horrible words.

Aspirin, ibuprofen, acetaminophen, an ice pack won't stop the pain.

An apology from you would have stopped the pain.

Leaving me alone in the first place could have prevented the pain.

I fake a smile for Mom.
I fake a smile for Dad.
I fake a smile for my little sib.
I fake a smile for my Grandma.
I fake a smile for my teachers.
I fake a smile for my counselor.
I fake a smile for my friend(s).
And when I look at my reflection,
I fake a smile to myself.

You hear laughter
I shed tears
You see beauty
I feel fear.

Please remember only the good things about me.
I was good at solving problems except for my own.
Please don't remember the bullying done to me.
Please remember to miss me.
Please never forget me.
Please.

WANTED

REPLACEMENT PARTS

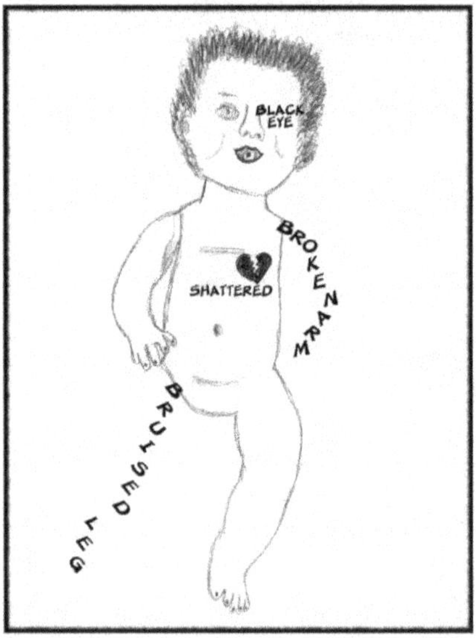

BECAUSE OF A BULLY

Seeking new parts to replace ones damaged by a bully. I need a new eye. My left one got punched and is now black and blue. I need a new arm. My left arm got broken when it was twisted behind my back. I need a new leg. My right leg is very bruised from repeated kicks. Finally, I need a new heart. Mine has been shattered into tiny pieces.

Star Light
Star Bright
The Pain They've
Caused Me
My Tears
Aren't Slight
I Wish I May
I Wish I Might
Not Have
My Heart
Broken 2Nite

Emotionally wounded
Emotionally cocooned
My soul has turned charcoal black
Pain-filled tears stain my face blue
Life has little meaning
I wish your hateful words had little meaning, too.

I'm done!

I'm going into my closet
But not for what you suppose
I don't care what I wear
This isn't about clothes.

I stand alone in the closet
Thinking over what next to do
Debating if I want it over
And wonder if you ever, even knew?

You think I am a waste of life, huh?
You suggest I should kill myself, already?
What if I did as you asked?
You'd probably say I was being petty

Why do you want me gone?
What did I ever do to you?
Why do you attack me online?
Why do you insist on not telling everyone the truth?

I don't know who you are
You won't tell me your name
Yet, you claim that you know me,
Call me an emo, loser and lame

You're not very original
Though you think you are
Hiding behind your computer
Causing emotional scars

Gutless, coward!

I've got an idea
Why don't you take my place?
You can walk down the halls
Get shoved and spit in the face

Let me type vicious lies, spread a rumor or two
Hey, keyboard commentator
Come and step into my shoes.

Whatever! Jerk!

I want to be somebody else.
I no longer want to be me.
I'd gladly be anybody.
Anybody, other than me.

I trusted you with a secret
You blabbed it to the whole school
Now everyone knows about it
You broke the pinky swear rule
I hate you!
Why did you pretend to be my friend?

If I could talk about it, part of me knows I would feel better.
Just wish I knew how to start.

I don't know who I am anymore.

A bully's recipe for Pound Cake:

2 Punches to the stomach
2 Slaps across the face
2 Kicks to the shins, one each
1 shout of *"Dork!"*
1 shout of *"Loser!"*
1 shout of *"Slut!"*
5 Others to yell the same

Mix it all together.
I lost my appetite for life.

I wish I could tell my parents what's wrong. But, I can't. They wouldn't understand.

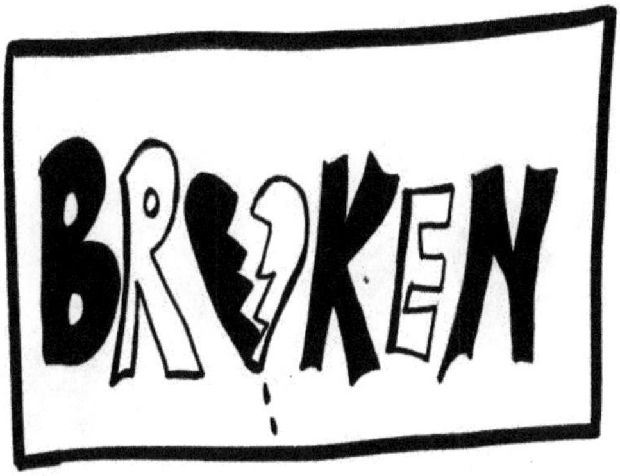

Depressed.
Tears.
Cast aside.
Incomplete.
Thrown out like trash.
Miserable.
Bruised.
Blue.
Bloody.
Frowning.
More tears.
Sad.
Lonely.
Done.

How are you doing?
Fine.

Are you lying?
Yes.

Why?
I don't know.

What's going on?
Nothing.

What's wrong?
Nothing.

Will you talk to me?
No.

Why not?
Why should I?

Because, I care.
No, you don't.
No one does.

A damn liar is what you are
Weekends were supposed to be fun
But, your hateful words took things too far

You called me a slut, a whore and a skank
My low self-esteem I now have you to thank

What you spoke was far from the truth
You knew nothing about me, so, where was your proof?

Being the new kid in town is never an easy road
You made sure the journey was bumpy for me
Ah, the vicious seeds you and your friends sowed

Running, running, running, your little lying mouths
The lies that spilled forth sent my entire reputation south

All I sought was acceptance, approval and love
But, you and your immature friends made certain each weekend was full of spite and shoves

A damn liar is all you will ever be
I did not have clear eyes before,
Oh, but now, how I do see

No more tears will I shed
No more wishing I was dead
No more wishing death for you
No more forgiving will I do

So, call me what you want
Think what you will
Now and forever
Your hateful lies mean nil.

I wish you would like me.
I wish you took the time to get to know me.
I wish I could tell you how much you have hurt me.
But, my mouth stays shut.
I say nothing.
Why bother.
It's obvious you don't care.
You just want to hurt me.
Why, I have no clue.
Wish I could understand what I possibly did to you?
For now, though, I think I'm just about through.

Everyone has a story to tell
Most are a journey straight into hell
Mine is no different
I'm willing to bet
It's the same as yours
Full of endless regrets.

I feel worthless
I feel blue
I feel like crap
How about you?

Oh, wait, that's right
How dumb of me to forget
You're so perfect and cool
Not like me, a social reject.

Please turn my upside-down heart right side up.
"How do I do this?", you ask.
Start giving me love.
Not repeated hate.

I am tired of being the exception to your social acceptance rule!

"Get out!"
"Piss off!"
"No one wants you!"
"Pathetic reject!"

Those nasty tunes of yours are blasted into my eardrums daily.

I wish the batteries that run your mouth would die.
I wish I could smash your verbal speakers.
I wish I could change your playlist.
I wish I could find the switch that turns you off.
I wish I could hear only silence.
While I continue wishing,
You, little bully, continue performing.

The world never sees the real me.
When facing my direction, it appears to be blinded by endless hate and disappointment.

A black eye and a broken nose
A twist to the arm
It's how my day goes

Bruises, slaps and kicks
My head punched so badly
I now feel awfully sick

Overwhelmed by grief
A razorblade cut penetrates my skin
Blood seeps out
So, begins my relief.

Perfect little bitch
Do as I say
Not as I do
You have no clue
How much I despise you, too
You're mean
You're nasty
You don't care what you do
How I wish you could be weak like me
How I wish I could be strong like you.

I was dead on arrival
The first day of school
A loud-mouthed bully
Found out I wasn't cool

I'm like, *"But you don't even know me"*
And the bully's like, *"I don't even care"*
I got shoved into some lockers
My new shirt received a tear

Kids pointed, laughed and stared
Feeling completely humiliated,
I ran home to hide in my lair.

Hur-ray! Hur-ray! Step right up!
Guaranteed this isn't a hoax.
What is so fascinating to see, you ask?
Me - God's perfect little joke.

Welcome to the show.
It's certainly one you don't want to miss.
Watch as I get kicked, punched and shoved.
Looking away will be hard to resist.

Enter the big Ol' bully
Who doles me a hearty black eye.
Watch it turn purple, ebony and blue,
as I hold it like a wimp and cry.

"Here comes the bearded lady", they shout,
as I walk from class to class.
Sometimes I am tripped in the halls
and I fall flat on my ass.

Other days, I'm thrust onto
a troller-coaster ride from hell.
Both hands raised high up in the air,
as I open my mouth and yell.

Living life under the big school tent,
I'm labeled a circus freak.
I don't exist to entertain and amaze you
But, I just thought I should finally speak.

Dear Bully,

I have a question I need to ask.
I promise it won't be a daunting task.
How did you know I was a loser before I did?

You're gonna miss me when I am gone. Right?

I give
You take
I love
You hate
I fail
You try
You laugh
I cry

Lost and not found
My self-esteem and confidence have disappeared
Maybe they're hiding underground
Constantly jeered at and ruthlessly smeared

I don't know where they are
Not sure if they ever existed
I do know I am scarred
I do know being bullied is twisted.

They're only words.
No, they're not!
They're verbal daggers
My soul you rip and shred

I am nothing.
A shell now.
An oxygen sucking loser.

Words don't hurt, huh?
You're right.
They destroy!

Your false projections
And ridiculous trajections
Have caused senseless rejections
Feelings of unnecessary subjections
I should have added some objections
Perhaps pushed for your ejection
Someone should have placed an interjection
Before my cries grew into introjections
I reside in complete dejection
Feelings of worthlessness are now repeated injections.

Someday, I will stand up to you.
Someday, I will not allow you to disrespect me anymore.
I wish someday was now.

I am a lonely girl.
I am a lonely boy.
Feeling like one of God's rejected, unwanted toys.

I don't feel loved.
I don't know what that is.
I only know hate.
I only know put downs.
I wish I knew what it felt like to hear someone say, *"I love you"*
instead of *"I hate you"* or *"I don't want you around"*.

I am so full of pain.
Why don't people like me?
What did I do?
Why won't anyone be my friend?
Why????

I'm nice and yet, I don't get treated nice.
What did I ever do?
What????
I'm so confused.

I feel so lost.

Why can't they see the real me?

I am,
a mistake,
a disgrace,
a screw-up,
a loser.

Who are you?
Bet I know.
Thankful you are not to me.

Making me weak
Such a clever technique
Never any shame
When calling me hurtful names

Picking on my size
Never caring to realize
How worthless you made me feel
The punches you threw, all too real.

My life feels like a blur
My pain is all too real
My head and heart concur
I wish no longer to feel.

death by hanging

Death by hanging has become a common solution to ending pain because of bullying. Many online sources claim, death by hanging is fast and painless. They are lying. The odds of breaking your neck right away are highly unlikely. That only happens in TV and movies.

Death by hanging is extremely agonizing and unpleasant. You will suffer. Here are some possibilities of what could happen to you during a hanging:

You might see flashes of light. This is no '*cool rave' effect*, as some websites describe. You are dying. Do you get it? DYING!

You might hear ringing in your ears.

You will lose consciousness, but it might not happen right away.

You will feel your organs shutting down. Organ failure hurts - a lot.

Your arms and legs will flail wildly about. This is an involuntary action. You cannot stop it or control it.

Your face will contort worse than Katie's, from the movie *"The Ring"*. By the time it is over, you may not even look like you.

Due to the violent shakes and convulsions your body experiences while being deprived of oxygen, the ligature you used to hang yourself might break. If this happens, you will drop to the ground like a rock.

You may or may not be dead at this point. You might still be alive, paralyzed or in a vegetative state. The outcome varies based upon how long your brain has gone without oxygen.

Eventually, your last breath will escape from your body.

You will pee and/or crap yourself before it is all over.

If you are a male, you might get an erection.

Your heart might beat for an additional 20 minutes. When it finally stops, you are officially dead.

You have endured a horrible physically painful experience to relieve emotional pain brought about by a bully.

Would you seriously consider ending your life because of a bully? Would you really allow someone to have that much power and control over your life?

No words, actions, behavior, or thoughts by another towards you, are ever worth ending your life over. Your life is not worth their power-trip.

Seriously, suicide IS NOT the answer to whatever problems or issues you have going on in your life. Circumstances are always subject to change. Instead of being a memory, choose to stick around and make memories.

Life is a precious gift.

Death is final.

You have a lot to give and the only way to do that is to live. So, live!

what is negative?

rumors
gossip
teasing
insults
threats
name calling
mean words
harassment

facts

there are 3 types of bullying

- ✓ mental
- ✓ physical
- ✓ emotional

Most assume physical bullying to be the worst of the three. Wrong. Though bruises may heal, broken hearts do not always do the same.

The pain borne from cruel, hateful words by far outweighs a fist punch. Words can cause destruction, emotional damage and sometimes provoke devastating life decisions, especially when coupled with social isolation. This often happens during bullying because words that have been weaved into lies and rumors.

The taunting phrase, *'Sticks and Stones may break my bones, but words will never hurt me'* has been proven to be nothing short of a cute saying wrapped up in a big lie. Words do indeed hurt.

'Folk Phrases of Four Counties' by G.F. Northall published the infamous *'Sticks and Stones'* taunt in 1894. Other versions include:

'Sticks and stones may break my bones, but words will never break me.' ~ The Christian Recorder (1862).

'Sticks and stones may break my bones, but names will never harm me.' ~ Tappy's Chicks: and Other Links Between Nature and Human Nature by Mrs. George Cupples (1872).

'Sticks and stones may break our bones, but words will break our hearts.' ~ All I Really Need to Know I Learned in Kindergarten by Robert Fulghum (1989).

'Sticks and stones may break my bones, but names will never down you.' ~ The Quiet One by The Who (1981).

'Life and death are in the power of the tongue' (Proverbs 18:21). Therefore, speak life (positive words) over someone, including yourself. Because to speak negatively over someone or yourself, serves only to generate pain, sorrow and the destruction of the spirit which lives inside each of us.

If you have been speaking ugly to someone or even to yourself, ask yourself these questions:

"Why am I deliberately choosing to speak death, when I can choose to speak life?"

"Why am I speaking bad about someone, when I can be speaking good about someone, including myself?"

"Why am I sowing rotten seeds that will leave my field with no crop, when I can sow healthy seeds that will have my field overflowing with many crops?" *(In other words, why am I robbing someone of joy, including myself, when I can be spreading joy?)*

did you know?

one:

Each year more than 160,000 students are absent from school due to bullying. Others are being removed from the system to get homeschooled.

two:

Bullying will always exist.

three:

How bullying situations are handled is changing. Stiffer laws and consequences for unacceptable bullying type behavior are currently being put into place to address this growing issue.

four:

Many people believe that *"A child's brain is not fully developed until they reach maturity so therefore, they know not what they do."* Wrong. Kids are taught the difference between right and wrong early in life. Bullying someone is wrong.

five:

When you think about it, bullying such as; spreading false rumors about someone is considered to be slander. Slander is a crime.

six:

Newspapers from various states are reporting cases where bullies are being charged for their actions. The Department of Justice (DOJ) has invested close to $2 million dollars for *'youth courts'* where middle school and high school kids act as judge, jury, prosecutor and defense in cases of bullying. They have the discretion to administer the appropriate punishment for the charge.

seven:

Today's bullying is very different than the bullying of yesteryear. Back in the day, when bullying became an issue, a kid was removed from one school and put into another and life was good again. Such is not the case anymore. This applies to homeschooling, too. The reason? Social media. The only way a child receives a break from the persistent badgering from their peers outside of school is to deliberately disengage from social media.

eight:

Bullying is capable of *"jumping over the pond"*. Thanks to the internet, bullying continues no matter where you are residing on the planet. There are several documented cases of bullied kids who moved to a new country to start over, only to have their past bullying issues discovered and spread all over their new school via social media.

nine:

Bullying *(especially cyber-bullying)* and intensified mental health issues either amplified or formed because of it can lead to suicide, especially for kids in their tweens and teens. The youngest case to date is that of a five-year-old.

ten:

Suicide is the wrong solution to end the pain you feel from being bullied. There is nothing worth ending your life over. Nothing! Your life matters. You matter.

eleven:

Did you know committing suicide due to bullying and intensified mental health issues either amplified or formed because of it, causes the following:

Devastated, heartbroken parents, who will struggle for the rest of their lives to try and understand why their child made such a harsh choice.

Siblings who will carry guilt for feeling they were not a better sister or brother.

Friends, who will think *'would have, could have, should have and if only'*.

Everyone left behind will wonder how they missed the tell-tale signs and experience what is known as, *"misplaced blame"*.

scoop

social-bullying: would you miss me?

Would you miss me if I went away?
Would you pause for a moment?
Beg me not to die, not to decay?
Is there someone, anyone, willing to say,
"Please, stay."
Nothing but silence.
Apparently, not today.

Why are people more appreciated and adored in death rather than in life?

T-Shirts plastered with photographs of a loved one gone too soon.
Faces stained with tears.
The sharing of memories.
Precious, heartfelt words rolling off tongues.
Confusion.
Anger.
Endless questions.

Amazing how we tend to take people for granted, isn't it? Especially a bully who intentionally generates anti-social behavior to their victim from themselves and others. They never dreamed their relentless ridiculing and isolation tactics could result in something as tragic as their target committing suicide.

Bullying is not just punching, rumor spreading or calling someone mean names.

Sometimes, people are bullied with silence. They are purposefully ignored or deliberately excluded from events that include their peers. They endure vicious rumors spread about them and are sometimes humiliated in public for amusement by their bully.

Other times, they are briefly acknowledged as either a cruel trick or when someone needs to use them for something. Otherwise, they are made to feel useless and unwanted by anyone for anything.

Social rejection is one of the harshest forms of punishment one human being can do to another. The emotional wounds run deep and take years to heal, if ever.

Victims of social bullying are often labeled *"worthless"* until they are gone. Only then do these sweet souls become encapsulated in acceptance, love and held in high regard.

Odd how they were hated, ignored and mistreated while breathing. Yet, suddenly they are loved, cherished, and memorialized after death.

Why? True guilt for those who caused the person to make such a harsh decision due to bullying. And, survivors guilt by those who maybe abandoned the victim due to peer pressure or felt they should have expressed their care for the person more than they did.

Victims of social Bullying often suffer in silence. They keep their pain well hidden. Some are so good at hiding it, even Sherlock Holmes, Inspector Gadget and Dick Tracy combined would have no clue what was going on.

Unfortunately, it seems only after a bullying victim is gone do the puzzle pieces fall into place. The subtle hints they may have dropped all along like bread crumbs on a trail, now light up brighter than an atom bomb. But, by then, it is too late.

Instead of someone reaching out and asking, *"Hey, would you like to hang out sometime?"* a lonely soul hangs alone in their room. Their body swaying silently side to side.

The question, *"Why didn't anybody like me?"* echoing inside their head until that last breath escapes their body. Alone in life. Alone in death. But, it does not have to end up this way.

never cause harm to yourself because of social bullying.

Haters are always going to hate someone or something for some reason. They have a problem. And, that problem is not you. Nor, does it have anything to do with you. The sooner you can get this – the sooner you can move past it and get on with your life.

Stop wasting your precious time caring, worrying or trying to prove yourself to be worthy of someone's time and attention who basically treats you like crap. You owe them nothing.

Believe it or not, the world is full of good people. You just happen to have had the misfortune of crossing paths with a jerk and some of his/her friends. If anything, be thankful you're not them. That's one way to look at it.

Stand strong and love and accept yourself, even if right now you feel like nobody else feels the same way about you. Do it for you.

Believe it or not there are people in your life who love you and want you around. They just need to speak up and let you know. Try taking the focus off the bully. You might then realize people are letting you know they care in their own unique way.

If you see someone being socially bullied, try and step outside of your comfort zone. Talk to the person. Stop caring what others around you might think if you do. Be a friend. Say, *"Hi"* or *"We're having an event, like to come?"* Compliment them on their wardrobe or if they are creative say, *"I really loved the short story you wrote and read in class today."* You never know how much your kind gesture might mean to them. It literally could be a matter of life or death.

Being bullied sucks. Stop caring what the bully thinks of you. Start working on developing some self-confidence.

to the bully: If you are socially bullying someone, stop it. No one likes a jerk. You might think they do. But, they don't. Keep in mind, you reap what you sow. You could just as easily find yourself being bullied, instead of being the bully. Don't be quick to scoff. It could happen. Instead of tearing someone down, your time might be better spent working on your own issues.

Being a bully is a lame lifestyle choice.
Stop being a jerk.
Start being a friend.

no angel am i

No angel am I
Heard sleeping around is a sin
Not ready to go to heaven
Won't dare let you boys win

My reputation got branded
Slut, whore, easy, bitch
The boys did call me by my name
Until I scratched their horny itch

How dare you boys spread rumors
How dare you boys scoff
My intentions weren't only
To get your worthless rocks off

I sought acceptance
I wanted love
I needed affection
Help from above

But, your hate fueled strife
Made me as popular as Hester Prynne
Slut shame comes with a price you know
Now, everyone knows where I've been

I got used, I got damaged
Lied to and mislead
A human mattress the boys called me
"She'll sleep with anyone", they said

The viral cyber campaign launched
Left destruction that can't be erased
No matter which State I move to
The world forever knows my face

Inbox offers from strangers
They keep pouring in
Lay on your back or kneel
Delete and into the trash bin

I'm not a Heavenly Angel
Not literally anyway
Because someone reached out
Someone begged me to stay

No matter what I've done
I'll always be better than you
The angels have given me wings of flight
I now rise above the hateful things you do

I'm free from the shame
My future is looking bright
My life has again become mine
I'm still here, now bathed in sunlight.

slut shaming

Per *Webster's Dictionary*, Slut Shaming is: the action or fact of stigmatizing a woman for engaging in behavior judged to be promiscuous or sexually provocative.

Slut Shaming has gained attention because of stories about teenagers harming themselves or committing suicide because of it, are being written in local newspapers and picked up by the national media.

People slut shamed by a bully are called, *'whore, slut, skank, tramp, bitch, ho, tease, loose, easy and nympho'.* A person being slut shamed has rumors spread about them. They also endure the exposure of any nude or semi-nude pictures or video of themselves being shared via text and/or cyberspace without their permission.

No one should ever be made to feel bad about themselves because of the number of sexual partners they have had, the nude or semi-nude pictures they sexted to someone or risqué video they may have willingly taken themselves or video unknowingly taken of them by someone else.

Is it wise to take nude or semi-nude pictures of yourself and then send them to your current love interest because they asked you to do so or because you felt like doing it? No. It is not a wise thing to do. It is also not wise to make risqué videos of yourself either.

Did you know most states consider nude and semi-nude material of someone under the age of eighteen to be child pornography? This applies to print as well as video.

Did you also know, if you are caught having possession of nude or semi-nude material (photos/video) of someone under the age of eighteen, you could be prosecuted and have your name put on a sexual predator list?

Did you know sending nude or semi-nude material (photos/video) of yourself to someone, whether requested or not, will not make them love you or serve to maintain their interest in you if they are pulling away?

Do you seriously want to risk having nude or semi-nude material (photos/video) of you floating around in cyberspace?

Taking such a drastic, demeaning approach will only gain you the wrong type of attention. Do it, and you flush your self-respect right down the toilet. Is having that person's attention worth giving up your self-respect?

Keep in mind, most relationships sour. I know that is hard to imagine being young and in love. But feelings do change. People fall out of love, just as quickly and easily as they fell in love.

When a relationship ends, sometimes one or both parties can be vengeful and cruel. Therefore, it is not a smart idea to record or snap nude or semi-nude material (photos/video) of you and/or your partner performing any type of sexual behavior. Because it can and most likely will be used against you.

The phrase, *"It will be for our eyes only"* is a LIE! Do not fall for it. Naughty stuff always has a way of finding a slut shaming audience. Keep that in mind if your partner says, *"Let's make a sex tape or send me some nude photos of you."*

Think before you act.
Think about the outcome.
Think about your ability to handle the consequences.
Think about your future.

We all do reckless stuff when we are young. No one is exempt from that rite of passage. However, regardless of the number of people someone sleeps with or the fact they may have sexted pictures or recorded risqué videos, no one should be singled out and humiliated for it. Especially to the point of choosing to end their life.

Let's not forget, it takes two to tango. So, if one person in the same scenario is going to be humiliated and slut shamed, perhaps the other participant(s) should step on up and claim their shame tag(s), too. If not, then they need to rethink their actions and behavior before being so quick to label someone a 'Hester Prynne'.

Unfortunately, because of social media, your wild past might linger. But, fear not. You have the power to overcome it, even if you cannot erase it. You can choose to move onward with your held high and not skulk.

Know this. It is easier than you think to be taken advantage of. The use of alcohol or drugs, smooth talkers who can be very persuasive, and your own burning desire to be popular and socially accepted, can all play a role in making not so wise choices. These are reasons, not excuses. And certainly not something you should feel ashamed of or be condemned for having done. Part of life is learning. We learn mostly from mistakes.

Remember, we all do things we regret. Add youth, inexperience, raging hormones and misguidance to the mix and you have a recipe for poor choices. Life is about improving, growing and developing ourselves into the person we want to be. The person we are destined to be.

What can drive a person to participate in promiscuous behavior boils down to three simple things; they seek acceptance, they want love and they need affection. Just so happens, they go about it the wrong way.

Did you know what is deemed 'slut shaming behavior' is not always about the act of sex itself? It is also about trying to fill a void from within. Something inside of the person acting out is broken.

The healing process of promiscuous behavior begins by first, figuring out the issue. The true root cause of why you are choosing to behave this way. Second, the issue, once figured out, needs to be addressed and sorted. As you heal, your self-respect will return, and you will start feeling good about yourself again. Despite what you may have done in the past.

My heart breaks each time I read another story about someone who chose to harm themselves or end their life because of slut shaming.

Being slut shamed hurts.
You think your life is over.
You think your life is ruined.
You think you will never be happy again.
You feel powerless because the pictures and/or video are out there in cyberspace and you cannot take any of it back.
You hate that everyone has seen the photos and/or video.
You feel embarrassed.
You feel humiliated.
You feel tired.
You hate yourself.
You hate everyone.
You are sick of being put down and made to feel bad about yourself.
You want it to stop.
You feel dirty.

question: *"How can I make it stop and go away?"*

answer: Develop an *"I don't give a crap"* attitude. I realize this is an easier said than done scenario. But, try. You have nothing to lose. And, quite honestly, it cannot get any worse than it is right now.

You have the power within you to rise above any mistake(s) made.
You have the power to conquer a bully.
You have the power to make changes for YOU.

Did you know if a bully fails to get a reaction out of you they eventually grow bored and move on? It might take some time, but they will move on. Just do your best to hang in there until they do. Do not give up. Do not let them win.

Keep your focus on what you can do about the situation at hand. Not what you cannot do about it. That is where the frustration lies. Feelings of powerlessness. Again, you are not powerless. You have just been made to feel that way. So, why continue allowing a bully to have that control over you?

please note: If you feel you have been sexually violated in any way, seek legal action immediately. Talk to your parents, a school counselor and the police.

If you simply made a bad judgement call, let it go. You cannot take it back. You cannot erase it. It does no good to churn your guts up about it. It is done. You can choose to change in your reaction or keep repeating the same depressing cycle. Again, your choice.

The bully wants you upset. Wants you hurt. Stop letting the bully have his/her way. Why give them that power over your life?

We have established the battle between you and your bully is over your damaged reputation. Control is what a bully wants. Now, is your time to take the control back.

When a bully slut shames you, you feel defeated. You have every right to feel this way because your reputation is being sullied. I am not saying you do not. But, if you hold your head high and display an *"I don't give a crap"* attitude, the bully is going to be left feeling confused. Your emotions are no longer being controlled by their cruel behavior. You are no longer reacting. You have taken the control back. You have the power.

No matter what life may throw at you, and believe me, it will throw some curve balls, always try and do your best to remain confident when handling the situation.

Be strong.
Be true to yourself.
Believe in yourself.
Love yourself no matter what.
We all wear battle scars in one form or another.
Nobody is perfect. NOBODY. Mistakes happen, and that is okay. It is how we learn, grow and move on.

rejected

"Emo!"
"Freak!"
"Weirdo!"
"Reject!"
"Nobody likes you!"
"Nobody wants you!"
"You don't belong!"
"Why are you still here?"

The all too familiar phrases repeatedly shouted out by a bully and his cohorts, while hurling empty soda cans and catapulting spit balls at a kid dressed in all black.

The kid, a sensitive, kind soul, quickly finds solace, hiding in the darkness behind a set of stairs, before the bullies can witness a steady stream of painful tears, certain to wash away the black eye make-up, placed heavily underneath his blue eyes. The kid sits down, pulls out his private journal and scribbles:

While I despise your cruel objections
And wish to initiate identical subjections
For you to feel your own hate-fueled injections
My thoughts now dwell on various life ejections

Live. Die. Live. Die. Live. Die. Live. Die. Live. Die.

Your relentless cruelty
has made this choice an obsession.
Which one I'll choose matters not
because according to you
My existence is that of a faceless reflection.

To survive in life, human beings require three basic things. Food, shelter and love. Without food, we starve. Without shelter we perish in the weather. Without love we feel rejected and alone.

According to the *Bible*, *"It is not good that Man should be alone" (Genesis 2:18).* It is almost impossible not to know what the unbearable pain of rejection and isolation from our peers feels like, if that statement were not true.

The emotion of loneliness we, as human beings, feel from time to time, lends merit to its verification. Though we may choose to be alone sometimes for assorted reasons, in the end, there is a significant difference between choosing to be alone and forced into loneliness.

Human beings are social creatures by nature. But, to get love, we must first learn how to give love. First to ourselves. Then, to others.

Let's look at the word reject from which the word rejection stems. According to *Webster's Dictionary*, the word 'reject' means; *to refuse to accept, consider, submit to, take for some purpose, or use.*

Rejection is one of the worst behaviors one human being can exhibit towards another. In college, Sociology 101, teaches the importance of belonging and being accepted within our species. Every human being craves it. No matter what their race, sex, sexual orientation, economic or social standing is.

Connecting with other human beings helps generate feelings of inclusion and belonging in the world. Again, it goes back to how human beings are wired. To not be alone.

People tend to believe if they do not fit in with a certain group or fail to meet a level of what society deems *"socially acceptable"*, there must be something wrong with them. Examples being;

they are not popular in school, are not earning enough money, are not married, they do not have kids, etc.

It is a downright tragedy how many good people are made to feel bad about themselves over societal expectations they may or may not have any control over.

When a person of any age faces social rejection, the fall-out can be very detrimental. Some never fully recover from this type of deliberate social isolation. They carry the painful scars for the rest of their lives.

Some are unable to cope with social rejection and end their suffering via suicide. Sad. Nothing or anyone or their opinion of you for that matter, is ever worth ending your life over.

People deemed *'social rejects'* by society, tend to become fixated upon what they feel is wrong with them to land them in that category. They do this to try and justify the rejection and/or make changes for the sole purpose of gaining social acceptance.

If you are being treated like a *'social reject'*, ask yourself these questions:

"Are there any changes necessary to make?"
"Am I basing the changes I want to make on a person's opinion about me?"
"Or, am I choosing to make changes based on my own self opinion without being influenced?"

'Social rejects' pick apart their hair *(the color, the style, the length or the texture)*, their make-up *(too heavy, too dark)*, their clothes, their body shape, their weight, their height, their eye color, their nose formation, how their lips look *(too skinny, too plump)*. Even the sound of their own voice can become an issue. Some go so far as to despise their birth name, and have it changed.

The list of *"things I hate about myself"* can run into infinity if not reigned in. It is very heartbreaking to watch someone tear themselves apart simply because they were made to feel socially unacceptable. A bully. Amazing how one person can come into another person's life like a wrecking ball and leave so much destruction.

"Okay. So, you spouted off all this advice. But, how do I become socially acceptable?" you ask.

For starters, stop criticizing yourself. Are you perfect? No. Do you deserve to be treated like a social outcast because of any imperfections? Never.

Tune out anything negative anyone says about you. Accepting their negative opinion of you is wrong thinking on your part. Whether you realize it or not, up until now you have been agreeing with their negative opinion of you enough to tear yourself down and question everything about yourself. Stop. You don't deserve it.

We all have faults. We all mess up. But, that is no reason to be singled out and treated like a social misfit just because one person gets the ball rolling based on their own judgmental opinion. Continue absorbing the negative garbage being said about you and it will destroy you.

Burn this into your thoughts so that it never leaves: *"There is no one else on the planet like you. You are not a perfect person, but you are not a mistake either."*

Instead of allowing another to tear you down, lift yourself up by embracing who you truly are. Love yourself. Accept yourself. Your opinion of yourself is what matters. Not a bully's. Or anyone else's.

If there is something about yourself you are not pleased with, change it. But, do it for yourself. Not because you are trying to gain social acceptance.

Those worthy of your time and love will love you back, faults and all. Those who choose to love you only without faults are shallow, narrow-minded people who are not worthy of your time, friendship or love. Forget them. Move on.

Listen, before you can expect anyone to love or accept you, you must first learn to love and accept yourself. Cliché, yes. But it is the truth.

shut the f-up!

Shut the F-Up
I don't care what you say
Shut the F-Up
Leave me alone, just go away

You pretend to be my friend
You pretend to care
Shut the F-Up
Erase that shocked stare

Shut the F-Up
I'm onto your lies
I know exactly who you turned into
your little bully spies

Shut the F-up
You'll not hurt me any longer
Shut the F-up
That's right, I'm getting stronger

Shut the F-Up
For it's my turn to speak
I said Shut the F-Up
You're the one who is pathetic
The one who is weak

Shut the F-Up
I'm not heartless like you
Shut the F-Up
I've spoken my peace
We're officially through

Shut the F-Up
I refuse to end my life
Shut the F-Up
I'm unconsumed with strife

Shut the F-up
I'm a winner and life chooser
Shut the F-Up
You sorry, little, bully loser.

i had no idea

Dear Mom,
Dear Dad,
I need to tell you
I'm feeling sad

You need to listen
For I need to speak
Things suck at school
My outlook on life has turned bleak

I'm being bullied, picked on, and teased
No matter what I try, my enemies are never pleased
I need your help for the bullying to end
I tried to handle it, but, by myself, I can no longer defend

The hatred, the lies, the rumors, the pain
At school or at home, it all feels the same
I need your strength, guidance, support and love
No judgements, anger, disappointments or shoves

Please be my parents
Don't be my friends
Help me, please, help me
Bring this bullying to an end

I love you.

Time and again the phrase, *"I had no idea"* is uttered by the parents of children who committed suicide because of being bullied or because their child was dealing with a mental health issue that became amplified or formed due to bullying.

They had no idea their child was being bullied. They had no idea their child was struggling with mental health issues. They had no idea their child was in so much pain. They had no idea their child was contemplating committing suicide. Sadly, they had no idea.

Because our society has become so busy and quite frankly, self-absorbed, it is easy to overlook those silent cries for help uttered by hurting children. If they ever even cry out for help at all. It is not uncommon for many to suffer in silence.

The world has evolved into a society of "*Go! Go! Go!*" We go to work. We go to school. We go to practice. We go to social events. We keep going until we think we cannot. And then, we go again. We have too or else we get left-behind. There is no rest for the weary. Nor, time for the hurting. This is what we have been led to believe. Guess what? It is all a lie. A lie that is costing us, mentally, physically and emotionally.

We no longer stop and smell the roses. Let alone water them. Our lives have tilted so far out of balance, along with our priorities.

Gone are the days of sit down meals and open discussions at the family table. Life now revolves around social media. There is no more talking. Only staring down at our individual phones, fully engaged in utter rubbish. Plenty of parents are just as guilty as their kids when it comes to this type of behavior.

This desensitizing behavior needs to stop. Now. Parents, put your phone down. Have your kid(s) put their phone down. Talk to one another. Really, talk. Openly. Frankly. Honestly. No judgements.

Listening to your kid smack their lips on fast food while rambling on about an after-school activity while sitting in the backseat as you drive them to the next event, does not qualify as an in-depth conversation with your child.

"I'm too busy" is no excuse. You made time to create your child. Now make time to be there for your child. No exceptions. It is important as a parent that you and your child look each other in the eye and have undivided attention. No distractions. Find out what is going on in your child's life. And, if you are the child – talk to your parents. Or a trusted adult at least. Stop holding in your feelings. You do not have to spend your life in pain.

Kids can be very good at hiding emotional pain. You might fire back with, *"I know my kid!"* Are you sure about that?

When was the last time you sat down with your child and had a real heart-to-heart conversation about things besides homework or the last sports game they played?

I can remember as a kid growing up, my family would sit down at the dinner table and talk about our day. My parents always took the time to talk to us kids no matter what was going on in their lives.

I can remember approaching my Dad in his workshop many times over the years and he would always stop what he was doing, pull out a stool and say, *"Have a seat, kid. Tell me what's going on."*

Because we had a bond, which both of my parents took the time to nurture, as kids, we felt comfortable enough to talk to our parents about anything and everything.

My parents were never nosy. They were in tune with their kids. They always knew when something was wrong. Even if they had to sometimes drag it out of us.

Because our parents had laid out that foundation of communication and trust when we were young, it helped us reach out to them when we were being bullied and when I especially felt overwhelmed and suicidal because of bullying.

A lot of parents make the mistake of trying to become their child's friend rather than being an actual parent. I am not saying that you cannot or should not be friends with your child. I think you should, once your child becomes an adult. But right now, they need guidance, love and protection. From you. The parent. Not their friend acting as if they are their parent when necessary.

I know it is natural for teens to rebel against their parent, but I also know teens can and will come to their parent, if they know their parent will be there with a hand stretched forth to help lift them up when they are down.

As a parent, please keep in mind that bullying can make a child feel very helpless, isolated, alone and like no one cares or understands what they are feeling or going through.

Often, a child will keep the bullying they are enduring to themselves out of fear of appearing weak, fear of retaliation from the kid who is bullying them, fear of rejection by their peers, fear their parent or another adult may judge them or punish them for being weak.

Please take the time to talk to your kid. Take the time and make the time to really get to know your kid.

Be a parent, not a friend. Your child needs you.

signs a child is being bullied

Unexplainable injuries
Lost or destroyed clothing/ books/electronics/jewelry
Feeling sick or faking illness
Changes in habits
Skipping meals or binge eating
Frequent nightmares
Difficulty sleeping
Not wanting to go to school
Declining grades
A loss of interest in schoolwork
Avoiding social activities
A sudden loss of friends
Decreased self-esteem or feelings of helplessness
Self-destructive behavior like running away from home, harming themselves or talking about suicide

signs a child is bullying others

Getting into physical or verbal fights
Have friends who bully others
Shows signs of increasingly aggressive behavior
Frequent visits to detention or the principal's office
New belongings or money that can't be explained
Blames others for their problems
Refuses to accept responsibility for their actions
Are competitive
Excessive worrying about reputation/popularity.

flip the bully script

Here is some information to help change a bullying situation around.

Put negative feelings aside and stop making them the center of your life.

You have every right to feel those negative emotions based on how terrible you have been treated, but the key, which is always over-looked is: YOU ARE IN CONTROL. Despite how it all looks, you are in control of your life and how you feel and react to situations.

The more you focus on the negative, the bigger and more out of balance feelings and thoughts can become.

You are a strong person.

Go look at yourself in the mirror. Really look. There is no one else on the planet like you. You are very special.
You are unique. God has a good plan and purpose for you in life. Say, *"I'm Okay"* - every day, several times a day, if necessary until it sinks into your heart and you believe it. The more you believe in something, the truer it becomes. How do you think the bully wore you down? Because you believed what they spouted off about you.

Replace the negative names with positive ones such as; smart, beautiful, handsome and a winner. Try and see yourself in a positive light instead of dogging yourself all the time. Eventually, others will begin seeing you in a positive light, too. It takes time, so be patient.

Take a time-out.

Stay off the internet for one week or even a month. Shut down your social media accounts. Once you remove the bully's ability to strike out at you online, you have taken the power back.

Let them type what they want. If that is how they choose to waste their time, let them do it. You do not have to waste your time reading their garbage. It's a choice.

Texting.

Ignore text messages from anyone other than your family or people you know are your friends. Delete any text message that comes in a bully. Do not read it. Delete it. The purpose of a text from a bully is to hurt you. So, do not give the bully the power.

If you are building a case against a bully, do not delete the messages. But, do not read them either. Give your phone to your Mom or Dad so they can read the messages from the bully and save them for law enforcement. It is okay to let your parents protect you.

You will never please everyone.

It is impossible. So, stop trying.

Get a "So what" attitude.

So, what, if there are pictures of you out there. You can't take them back. Learn from it. Do not do it again. Move on.

And please stop being hard on yourself if you sexted someone who then shared your private photos. You are not the first person to make this mistake. Unfortunately, you won't be the last one, either. Everything is going to be okay. It will take time for things to simmer down. But they will.

Do not give up on yourself.

Believe you can survive being bullied and you will.

If you act like you don't care on the surface, *(even though inside you do care)*, the bully is robbed of the thrill they are seeking by causing you pain. Once a bully realizes they cannot get a reaction out of you, the game is over for them. You win. They lose and move on.

Ignore the rumors spread about you.

Never allow anyone to make you feel pressured into proving or defending who you are. Let them say what they want about you. So, what. You never have to prove anything to anyone about yourself to win approval.

Ignore the bully while at school.

This might not be possible all the time. But, try your best. Nothing upsets a bully more than to have their power taken away. You accomplish this task by simply ignoring anything they say to you.

What if a bully is beating on you?

If you have a bully who hits you, make sure you are never alone. You should also tell your teacher and your parents if you are being physically attacked. No one deserves to be hit.

Telling someone you are being bullied does not make you a tattletale. You were not put on this earth to be someone's punching bag. That is called ABUSE. Abuse of any kind is never okay. Tell an adult if you are being abused by anyone, please.

Talk to a trusted adult about being bullied.

Talking to an adult about being bullied is wise because believe it or not, they may have been bullied too and have good advice to share.

Again, you are not a tattletale. You are seeking a reasonable solution to a problem. There is no shame in getting help for a problem. And being bullied is a problem.

Tell an adult if you are feeling suicidal or having bad thoughts about yourself.

This applies whether you are being bullied or not. There is nothing wrong with getting help. There is nothing wrong with seeking out advice. It does not make you weak. It makes you brave.

Please do not keep those bad feelings to yourself. The longer you hold bad feelings in, the worse they become.
So, talk to a responsible adult about them NOW!

Take the focus off yourself.

You think your life is bad? I can guarantee you, someone out there has it worse than you and would give anything to be in your shoes. For real. Everyone thinks their issues are MAJOR. To most, they are. And some may very well be. But, if you were to take a room full of people and stack their issues up against yours, you might be surprised at how different your situation looks to you now. Maybe you might realize that it is not as bleak and hopeless as you thought. Stay focused on the positive things. Let go of the negative. You are in control of your life, your destiny.

In the end.

Everyone makes mistakes. Mistakes are learning experiences on what not to do again. They are not a means to continually punish ourselves, nor allow anyone else to punish us for them, either.

Things happen in life, whether good or bad. They do not define who you are as a person. Please remember it was/is one moment in your life. Not your entire life.

You have a long life to live. Don't quit now. Give yourself a chance. I think you're worth it. You should, too.

put the right foot forward

Right foot. Not Left
I've made my choice
Hateful words matter not
Now hear my strong voice.

We have choices every morning we wake up. For example, we can choose to get out of bed in a good mood or a bad mood. The circumstances matter not. It is how we choose to handle the things in our life, no matter how pleasant or unpleasant they might be.

The same decision making can also be applied when hearing rumors spoken about yourself or other people. You can choose to believe the rumors or not.

You can also choose to believe positive things about yourself such as: amazing, creative, happy, beautiful, strong, and loving. Or, you can choose to focus on the negative things from a bully, such as: loser, dumb, ugly, dork and slut.

You always have the power to choose which path you want to walk. You never have to tolerate negativity in your life unless YOU decide to do so. It is your choice.

One way to look at is like this. Just because the mailman brings you a package, does not mean you have to accept what is inside the box.

Make the decision today that from now on you are going to believe only good things about yourself and no longer focus on negative energy from a bully.

What you think of yourself is so important. More than you may realize. You need to stop caring what a bully thinks about you. You do not need their approval to be acceptable in this world. You are acceptable. Here. Now. Just as you are. You have value, a purpose, a plan. Never allow anyone tell you otherwise. If they should, know they are lying.

Here are some questions to consider that might help skew any negative perspective you may have of yourself due to someone's unfortunate opinion of you.

"Who put a bully in charge of deciding you were not socially acceptable?"

The answer will surprise you.

You did.

"But how?" You ask.

The moment you chose to believe their negativity about yourself. Fear not though. The good news is you can turn it around.

"How?"

By choosing to focus on the positive things in your life. Even if it is only one minor thing. It still counts. And, by blocking the bully; mentally and emotionally.

"How do I accomplish this?"

You just decide to do it and follow through. It might not be easy at first. Mind of matter never is. But, with practice and dedication, it will become a new and improved way of thinking which will serve to benefit you in the long run.

You can defeat your bully and neigh Sayers. Maybe you never realized it until now or maybe you felt like you were not strong enough. But you now know you have strength, power and control over your life.

A bully cannot have power over you unless you allow it. They only want the power because they are nothing more than insecure people trying to appear powerful. Once you recognize this, their power is stripped away.

You must decide - right here -right now:

" Do I want to take the control and power back in my life?"

Every day is full of choices. Which foot do you want to choose to lead with, starting now?

I have no doubt you will make the RIGHT choice.

quick chat for girls

Maintain self-respect in all areas of your life. Never allow anyone to pressure you into doing anything you feel uncomfortable doing. Especially in the hopes of gaining their approval. For example: doing drugs, drinking, having sex or sexting.

If you have been having sex, simply in the hopes of winning someone over - STOP. You will not win. That is not the way. If someone truly cares about you and really loves you, they will treat you with respect, acknowledge any boundaries you set in place, and never pressure you into going against your morals and values.

If someone cannot treat you with the respect you rightly deserve, you do not need them in your life. Promptly show them the door. And never look back.

In the end, sleeping around to gain popularity, social approval or what you believe to be love, will you get nothing but a bad reputation and a broken heart. Ask yourself if it is worth the sacrifices you must make.

You will not be popular in the way you think.
You will gain a negative reputation.
You will most likely get slut-shamed.
You will not feel good about yourself on the inside.
You will not win over *"Prince Charming"* or his friends.
Sometimes sacrifices are worth making. This, however, is not one of those times.
Do not do it.
And, if you have been doing it, stop. Right now.
It is never too late to make a change.

As a female, but more importantly a human being, you never deserve to be used, mislead or *'Slut-Shamed'* no matter what you have done.

The right person will come into your life and treat you like a queen, a lady, when the time is right. It is better to hold out, then to hold on to something that is no good for you. The right person will not treat you like a booty call. If a person treats you this way, dump them. They are no good for you.

Did you know loose behavior is likely the result of misplaced feelings, not because someone is *'easy'*?

Believe it or not, you might be seeking acceptance, wanting love, needing affection or trying to fill an empty void inside of yourself. Or, you might be reacting to some type of trauma you are either consciously aware of happened to you or something that was done to you that you cannot recall. You just know something is not quite right down inside. Recognizing there might be an issue is the first step towards getting it sorted and making changes in your life for the better. Do not lose hope. There is always hope in every situation.

Never compromise your morals or values for anyone. Sacrificing your self-worth is not worth it. Value yourself and the right guy will value you in return. Be a virtuous woman. You are a precious jewel worthy of special treatment. Never settle for anything but the best treatment.

"When will I know it is the right person?"
"You'll just know."

Watch for the frogs on the journey to meeting your Prince.

quick chat for guys

Being a tough guy has its time and place. Acting like a bully is not one of them. Be considerate of other people's feelings. Treat people with respect, the way you would want to be treated. Why choose to do wrong when you can choose to do right?

When it comes to the ladies, remember they are someone's sister, daughter and mother, should you become tempted to 'slut-shame' or disrespect them in anyway.

One day you might have a daughter. Would you want your daughter to be disrespected and mistreated by someone? The answer is, *"No!"*

Never be afraid to open-up to someone if something is eating away at you. Share what is going on inside. Unburden yourself from that weight. There is no need to carry it around.

In society, men are taught to hide their feelings. This is wrong teaching. It is okay for a man to feel and express his emotions. It is okay for a man to cry. Crying can be healing. This does not make the man weak or any less of a man for that matter.

If you are ever feeling confused about things in your life or how to handle a situation, please do not be afraid to open-up and talk to a trusted adult about it. Let it out. Do not hold it in.

Avoid being concerned with how others might see you. A real man stands proud and own who he is. He does not care what others think. A real man deals with situations. A real man does not run like a coward. A real man never cares others might think about him. A real man has self- respect and shows respect to others.

You have one life to live. Live it the way you see fit. But, keep in mind to also live it in a way that does not deliberately cause harm or pain to others.

quick chat for both

Ignore the haters.
Plan your future. *(Yes, you have one.)*
Stay focused on school.
Ignore the negativity.
Do not be led by confusion.
Nor distracted by scattered thoughts and emotions.
Keep your attention centered on your goals.
What goals?
Graduating. Then college. Then a career. Etc.…

Yes, school might be a drag because of bullying and other teen/life issues. There are also break-ups and failed grades. No shame in either. It is a part of learning and developing into the person we want to be.

Try developing a better attitude. You have a future to plan for. Whether you realize it or not, school is only a temporary stop. It is not the whole journey. Even though it might feel like it right now.

Where do you see yourself a year from now?
Where would you like to be a year from now?
How are you going to make it happen?

Where do you see yourself five years from now?
Where would you like to be five years from now?
How are you going to make it happen?

Where would you like to go to college?
What grades do you need to make to get accepted into the college of your dreams?

How do you plan to make your dreams come true?

Don't feel overwhelmed. Planning for a future is exciting. It gives purpose. Something to look forward to working towards, whether you get there or not. Or, something better comes into our lives along the way. It does not matter if you fail. What matters the most – you try.

If time permits and you can manage to keep up your grades, consider getting a part-time job doing something you enjoy. You can use the money earned to buy a car or put it towards college expenses. Having a job and saving money for something is a great self-esteem booster. It feels good to earn things in life. Not have them handed to you.

Despite the negative parts of being a teenager in high school that feel like your whole life, try and get some enjoyment out of those youthful years. They can be some of the best times of your life if you so choose. They only happen once. So, make the most of them.

Do not worry about racking up random hook-ups, getting married or having a baby right now. Save those moments for when you are more mature and settled. This is your time. It is okay to be a little selfish and focus on yourself during this time.

Keep your eye on your goals. Get something positive going for yourself first before you share it with someone else. Do not be afraid to pursue that career you want or eventually buy/rent a place of your own *(when you are old enough to legally move out)*. Go for it.

Take this valuable time to get to know yourself during these *'growing years'*. Stop worrying about trying to be something you are never going to be no matter how hard you try. Perfect. Being perfect is an unrealistic goal. To avoid this trap set by your bully, you must learn to accept yourself, flaws and all. And realize, everyone has flaws. EVERYONE.

Love yourself. And, always be yourself no matter what.
Never change who you are to please someone else. Stand by your boundaries. Never settle for anything less.

You are special. You are you. There is no one else like you on the planet. Hold your head up high and be proud of who you are. Of who you are evolving to be.

Make your mark in the world. But, check any ego issues at the door. Being proud does not mean acting like a diva or a jerk.

There is an old Latin quote which goes, *"Illegitimi non carborundum"* which means, *"Don't let the bastards grind you down."*

You can make it.
You will make it.
You are making it.
I am proud of you.
You should be proud of you, too.

Which secrets to keep
Which secrets to share

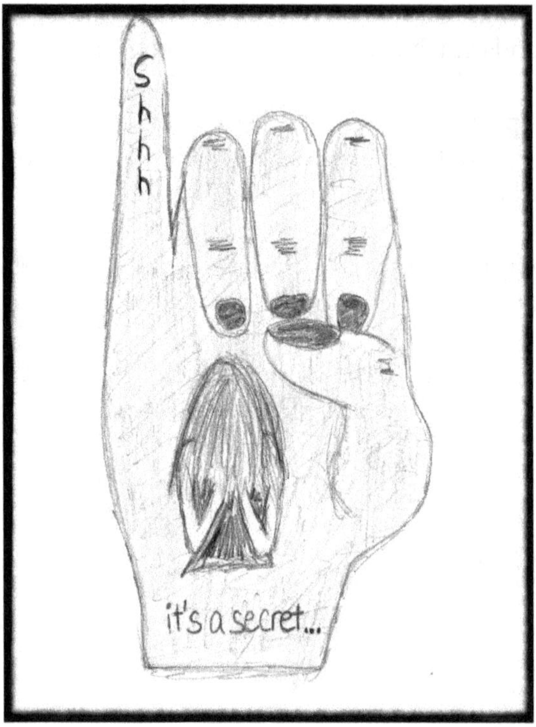

Friends tell each other secrets all the time.
Who their crush is.
What they think of their parents.
What they dream about.
A pinky-swear. A tick-a-lock. And, the secret remains between them forever.

But, sometimes a friend might tell a secret that should be shared with a trusted adult and not be kept a secret.

Why? Because certain secrets can literally be a matter of life or death.

these are secrets to share with a trusted adult:

*if someone is talking about killing themselves.
*if someone is talking about cutting themselves.
*if someone is talking about feeling depressed.
*if someone is talking about crying all the time.
*if someone is talking about quitting/giving up on stuff.
*if someone is talking about hurting others.

The right thing to do if you know of someone who is talking about hurting themselves is to tell a trusted adult about it. You are not a snitch if you tell. You are a lifesaver. You are brave. You are a hero. You are a friend.

Do not worry if you lose your friendship with the person whose secret you shared. Even if it might seem like the end of the world to you at the time. Better to lose the friendship for a while and save their life than to sit back and do nothing. Hopefully with time and treatment, they will see what a loyal, caring friend you truly are.

A person who goes the extra mile for another is a rare find. A treasure. You are very blessed if you have a friend like that in your life. Someone who 'has your back'.

Words may hurt. But, they can also save a life. Do not be afraid to speak up. Be a friend. Tell if you know.

words do hurt

We have all heard the saying, *"Sticks and Stones may break my bones, but words will never hurt me"*.

I suppose that depends on who is saying the words, what words are being said and why they are being said. Some will argue the classic saying holds true. Others will strongly disagree and state, *"Words most definitely hurt and can cause lifelong damage to a person."*

From birth, until death, people will be speaking into our lives. Some will speak positive. Some will speak negative. And some, will fall under the category of constructive criticism. Those people have intentions of helping one to become the best they can be, especially when that person fails to see potential within themselves.

It is only natural we revel in joy with positive words. Positive means acceptance and approval. But, when the words spoken to us are negative, rejection and hurt feelings surface.

We either consciously or unconsciously, seek acceptance and approval from family members, friends, co-workers, a crush and even a stranger we pass along the way.

Society has falsely taught us to automatically accept and value other peoples' opinions of us over our own personal feelings about ourselves. No questioning why. No exceptions to how. It is wrong thinking and very destructive to our self-esteem.

What other people think of us matters so much it can affect our mood and how we think and feel about ourselves 24/7. What an unnecessary stress and burden to carry.

When a person's opinion of you comes to a point where you turn on yourself, that is a red flag. A warning to stop and reevaluate that person and their purpose in your life. It is also a time for you to reevaluate your own thinking and to discover why you are allowing one person to have so much control over your life to the point where you are becoming your own worst enemy.

"How do I change the way I have been thinking about myself?" you ask.

Sociology classes teach us that people need people. The *Holy Bible* even states it in *Genesis 2:18*, *"It is not good for man to be alone."*

Before we were born, we were loaded with expectations: to walk, to talk, to go to school, have friends, to graduate, go to college, have a career, get married, have a family, retire, become a grandparent and finally live out our golden years playing checkers and doing prune juice shots at a nursing home until our time comes to sprout wings and hold a harp.

Should we fail to participate in those areas of false expectations, we are doomed to feel like a failure and an outcast. Again, this is wrong thinking and very destructive to our self-esteem.

Because of the ingrained need for approval and acceptance from others, it can be incredibly damaging to be bullied and socially isolated. Receiving this type of harsh treatment goes against everything we were taught.

Animals, insects, and humans survive within a *"pecking order"*. Someone is the leader. Someone is always fighting to take their place. This natural order of things does not mean bullying is an acceptable behavior in which to achieve said coveted position. There is a clear difference between being a strong leader and being a bully.

A leader should be respected, not feared. A leader should never bully.

A bully is not respected and is feared. A bully is not a true leader.

A bully does not lead. They control another by breaking them down through mental, emotional and physical duress. Bullying is about humiliation and submission. Not leadership.

If you are following a bully, now might be an appropriate time to reevaluate why you are doing so and to stop.

If you have been allowing another person's opinion of you to override your own opinion of yourself, now might be an appropriate time to stop and reevaluate why you are allowing it to happen.

You've made me cry
Only you know why
Seems no matter how hard I try
My words keep getting twisted into lies
You might be slick, even a little sly

But, I have a secret.

So, take a breath, let out your annoying sigh
You will not defeat me, make me quit life and die

To your cruelty, torment, negativity I say,
"goodbye."

To my joy, happiness and positive outlook I now say,
"hi!"

being you-nique is cool!

Weirdo. Freak. Emo. Strange. Odd. Geek. Misfit. Samples of hurtful insults often hurled by a bully. But, what if you looked at those words in a new way? Instead of horrible, how about *"Unique"* or, even better, *"YOU-nique"*, instead?

If no one has told you before, I am going to now. Being *YOU-nique* is chic. Being yourself is good. Not bad as a bully may have been portraying it to be.

Tim Burton's film, *Frankenweenie,* features a character named *"Weird Girl"*, along with her clairvoyant pussy cat, *Mr. Whiskers.*

Frankenweenie's Wiki page describes *Weird Girl as,* "Someone who does not fit in well with other kids. She delivers ominous pronouncements in a monotone voice. Her cat, *Mr. Whiskers,* is a constant companion. *Weird Girl* and *Mr. Whiskers* both have an unnerving, unblinking stare. *Weird Girl* loves to share *Mr. Whisker's* dreams to those whom he dreamt about."

Weird Girl is never bothered by the social bullying she receives from the other kids. *Weird Girl* embraces who she is, from her large staring eyes, to her monotone voice, to her psychic abilities to read *'signs Mr. Whisker's leaves in the litter box'.*

Weird Girl is unique. Her style of clothes. Her hair. Her voice. Her personality. Everything about her is kooky and quirky, but unique and adorable at the same time.

Weird Girl does not hide who she is. She could care less what others think of her. She displays her unique personality traits proudly. She never allows anyone to make her feel ashamed of who she is just because they may take issue with it. She is clever enough to recognize that is their problem. Not hers.

Being unique does not have to be a curse. It can be a blessing. It can also be fun, too. The choice on how you manage your uniqueness is yours alone no matter what unique qualities you adorn:
Your physical appearance (eyes, nose, mouth, hair, height or weight).
Your clothes.
Your voice or manner of speech.

Your personality.
Your quirks.
Your taste in TV/Movies/Music.
Whatever.

Never give someone the power to make you feel bad about your uniqueness. Embrace it. Do not hide it, feel ashamed or put yourself down about it, either.

If someone doesn't appreciate your *YOU-niqueness*, that is their problem. Let them keep it. They are most likely jealous and wish they had the guts to stand proud and be who they are, wear what they want, say how they feel, etc...

Thought stated already, it bears repeating. There is no one else like you. You are special and here for a great purpose. You are not here to be abused physically, emotionally or mentally by someone who does not understand or appreciate you and your uniqueness.

Weird Girl's quotes from the movie *'Frankenweenie'* read, *"Mr. Whisker's had a dream about you last night. If Mr. Whiskers dreams about you, it means something big is going to happen."* That something big could be you deciding to love yourself, to accept yourself, to be proud of yourself, to embrace who you are.

Be yourself no matter what anyone else says. Being YOU-nique is chic.

question…

"Who put a bully in charge of deciding being yourself wasn't good enough?"

reply…

You did once you caved into their pressure and hid your uniqueness. Do not feel bad about yourself for doing so.

solution…

Brush off their hate. Brush off any self-hate you are feeling.
Love and accept yourself just as you are.
Change for no one.

bullied kids getting homeschooled are earning an "e" for emotional pain

Natural parental instincts are to protect your child. Especially when it comes to the issue of bullying. No one wants to see their child in pain, whether it be physical, mental or emotional. Witnessing your child being hurt is one of the worst feelings for a parent to experience.

So, what is a parent to do if their child is getting severely bullied at school?

Parents - talk to your child and find out what is going on. Kids can be secretive and may not be forthcoming with their situation. It is not uncommon for victims of bullying to hide their pain due to feelings of shame, helplessness, depression and frustration.

Be the parent, not the buddy to your child right now. You must open the lines of communication and dialogue with your child. A child in pain needs unconditional love, security, strength, wisdom, guidance, reassurance and a solid foundation that only you, their parent, can provide. They need you now more than ever.

Kids – do not be afraid to talk to your parents or a trusted adult about your feelings, no matter what they may be. For every problem, there is a solution. You do not have to keep feeling bad. Nor do you have to silence your pain by ending your life. That is not the answer. Do that and you lose. They win. Talk to someone. You will feel better.

Parents - visit your child's school and find out what they *(teachers, principal, counselor, superintendent)* know about the bullying happening to your child. Cooler heads prevail. So, as much as you may want to lash out because your baby is being hurt, reign it in. Again, for every problem, there is a solution.

If you discover the school is unaware your child is being bullied, make them aware of it. Provide calm, reasonable conversation and any proof; text messages, emails, etc.... Find out what the school plans to do about the bullying and make sure they follow through. You will probably need to be proactive in this situation with periodic talks with your child, meetings with the Principal and/or teachers to ensure the bullying issue is getting resolved.

Getting proactive with the school system may or may not solve the problem. It is not uncommon for many parents in your situation to be left feeling frustrated with the entire situation and get left with no other option, but to homeschool.

Many parents are opting to homeschool their children due to the school system's failure to prevent their child from being bullied. Homeschooling is being viewed as the best solution to this ever-growing problem. In some cases, it has proved to help resolve bullying issues when the school failed to do so.

However, no system is perfect. Homeschooling can raise additional problems for a bullied child: social-isolation, an inability to develop coping mechanisms to handle challenging issues and not dealing with the existing emotional fall-out from being bullied.

One critical area often overlooked before homeschooling even begins is existing emotional damage done to the child by the bully. No amount of homeschooling will ease those hurt feelings. Be aware, removing your child from a bullying situation does not remove the pain caused by the bully. Professional help may be needed.

Protection and privacy have a fine line between them that must be crossed sometimes, for the right reason. Bullying is one such reason. Parents have the right to monitor their child's computer and phone activity. Kids need to be told why it is happening and assured it is not an invasion of privacy, but for their protection.

Being a parent today is no easy task. Neither is being a kid. Talk to your child. Hug them often. Tell them you love them, and you are there for them no matter what. Keep in touch with what is happening in their life whether you choose home schooling as the solution to your child's bullying issue or not. A bullied child needs support and assurance to help them overcome the damage done to them because of the bullying. Be there for them.

don't let them break you!

The thought of High School reminds one of the John Hughes flick, *'Pretty in Pink'*, and the creatively dressed character Andie, played by actress, Molly Ringwald.

Andie was a girl from the poor side of town who got bullied by the rich kids at her school because she was different. She was a talented designer and a caring person who never judged anyone for anything. She accepted people as they were. Rich. Poor. Ugly. Pretty. It did not matter. She never judged. Her heart was pure. She was real and could not be bought or impressed by money.

The rich kids knew down inside Andie was a better person than they would ever hope to be. They had plenty in materialistic items, unlike Andie. But, also unlike Andie, they lacked character and integrity. Two things money cannot buy. They resented and bullied Andie for this reason.

A classic line Andie quoted from the movie, when her Dad asked her why she was still going the prom despite having been dumped by her date *(who happened to be a rich guy)*. Her simple reply was; *"I just want them to know that they didn't break me."*

Social media, daily interactions at school or after-school events have made bullying almost impossible to avoid nowadays.

Victims are being broken to the point where they are turning the malice vented by the bullies, at themselves. It is called self-hatred. Self-hatred seeks to destroy. The good news is, you have the power within you to prevent it from happening.

A new school year brings about the perfect time for changes. Rise above the nonsense of put-downs and gossip. Those things are driven by jealousy and serve only to keep you distracted from what is important in life. Your future.

You have an amazing future waiting for you. Do not allow bullying to destroy all you have worked so hard for: good grades, getting into the college of your dreams, etc.… Stay focused on what is important. Your life. Your future. Your goals.

Always strive to be the best you that you can possibly be. But, do it for you. No one else. You do not ever have to prove anything to anyone. Even though it might come across as being narcissistic, it is not. This is not about a big ego, acting like a diva or thinking you are better than anyone else.

Do you want to know the secret to avoid someone destroying your self-esteem?

For, every tear down someone gives you, give yourself two build-ups. Stop taking crap. Stop accepting what a bully says about you as gospel. For example: if your bully says, "You are stupid." You automatically reject what they said before it has a chance to take root and say to yourself, "No. I am smart. I am somebody."

Unfortunately, people say and do horrible things to one another all the time. The important thing to remember is how you respond to what is said or done. I say, *"Be strong and rise above it!"*

The only way someone can break you is if you give them the power to do it. So, don't.

being bullied made me become a bully. Why?

The question, *"How did being bullied turn me into a bully?"* has been asked time and again by those who have been bullied.

Anger, insecurity, jealousy, hatred for others, hatred for self are just a few of the many reasons why someone chooses to become a bully. Then there are those who start life full of love and compassion for others. But, because of bullying, the love and compassion sours and they end up becoming a bully, too.

No matter how bullying starts, in the end it always boils down to one objective. Control. Bullying is nothing more than the need to control another to help the bully feel better about themselves. It really is that simple.

A bullied person, who then becomes a bully, not only carries the pain caused by their bully, but also the guilt of bullying others. Why? Because no matter how much the love and compassion for others seems a distant memory, down inside, being a bully goes against their nature: to love and have compassion for others.

The fact that a bullied person evolves into a bully is not their fault. They are what is called, '*A Victim of Circumstance*'.

Being a VOC is not a viable excuse to bully. In fact, there is no viable excuse for bullying another. Period. However, if a VOC had not been bullied, they most likely would have never developed into a bully themselves.

Unfortunately, hurtful circumstances can cause a VOC to make bad choices when it comes to the treatment of others. But, if a VOC feels guilt over bullying another, clearly, they still have a heart and a conscience. They are just overloaded with pain and acting out because they do not know what else to do. They are overwhelmed and confused by too many emotions.

It is perfectly understandable if VOC wakes up one day and feels guilty for their past behavior towards others. They turned into the very type of person they spent years fighting so hard against.

"What can one do to ease the guilt and shame that comes with being a VOC bully?"

Recognize the past is the past. As much as we all wish we could go back and undue stuff, it's impossible. Let it go. It's over. Done with. Gone. Move on. You cannot change it. So, stop exhausting yourself physically, emotionally and mentally

Forgive those who have bullied you. Forgiveness is often the hardest thing in the world to do, but also, the most rewarding for your own self-preservation. Forgiveness is a very important, necessary step. By forgiving the one or ones who did you wrong, you will begin to heal from the pain. You may never forget what was done, but through forgiveness, it won't sting like it used too.

Walking in forgiveness, rather than in bitterness, anger and hatred is best. Negative emotions do nothing more than cause destruction in health and other areas of your life. Is a bully worth doing that to you?

Stop giving your bully the control.

If you became a VOC, forgive yourself for the bullying that you did. You were a victim. Both in bullying and of circumstance. It was not your fault what happened. Yes, you may have done horrible things, but the time has come to let it go, forgive and move on.

Do not be afraid or shy to talk to someone about your feelings: a parent, a teacher, a doctor, a school counselor, a pastor or a trusted adult in your life. Keeping bad or sad feelings bottled up inside is not healthy for your mental or physical well-being. So, talk to someone. Let those feelings out before they smother you.

Forgive the bully, forgive yourself and then, move on.

8 miles of bullying

One day, I channel surfed upon the movie, *"8 Mile"* starring *Eminem, Kim Basinger, Mekhi Phifer* and the late *Brittany Murphy.*

I had not seen *"8 Mile"* since its release back in 2002. My timing could not have been better. *Eminem's* character, *B-Rabbit* and his rival, *Papa Doc*, were about to battle for the title of best rapper in Detroit.

Forget for a moment these two Actor/Rappers are playing characters. Forget that the rap was pre-written, based on scripted events in the movie.

What made this scene in *"8 Mile"* stand out was the fact that *Eminem/B-Rabbit*, took the power away from *Papa Doc* – a bully.

In the movie, the MC flipped a coin and *Papa Doc* had the option to go first or pass. He passed.

See, *Papa Doc* thought he was slick by letting *B-Rabbit* take the mic first. *Papa Doc's* cocky, bully attitude allowed him to falsely believe he was going to win simply by ragging on *B-Rabbit* using typical bully put-downs.

Watch the movie *'8 Mile'* for *Eminem/B-Rabbit's* rap off scene mentioned. You can see for yourself how *B-Rabbit* begins with telling the crowd the negative things he knows *Papa Doc* is going to say about him. But then there is a twist. *B-Rabbit* goes on to share things about *Papa Doc.* He then tosses the microphone over to *Papa Doc*, who is left speechless. Why? Because *B-Rabbit* took the power back.

The character *B-Rabbit* owned the good, the bad, and the ugly about himself. He acknowledged all the things in which *Papa Doc* found fault. That is how he took the power back. Once

Papa Doc's power was stripped away, he had nothing. He could no longer hurt *B-Rabbit.*

What makes a bully appear strong and more superior is their ability to deflect their own issues. That is how they become the bully and not the bullied. But, underneath the tough exterior they front, is nothing. They are a weak, pathetic and lost person with issues that will most likely require professional help to fix.

Despite being a *'jerk'*, a bully should never be made to feel shame or be ridiculed for their issues. Do that, and you are not better than them. Look, we all have issues – some just happen to be better at handling them and not taking them out on others.

Even though a bully may know WHAT they are doing to you, they do not know WHY they are doing it to you.
They may not even know WHY they feel hate for you.

It is not entirely impossible to believe down inside, they may like you and respect you. But, either they don't see it because they are so consumed with jealousy and envy. Whatever a bully's problem with you might be, remember they have the problem. Not you.

Do not allow yourself to feel like you must pick up their mantle of hate, self-loathing and despair in return. And never turn on yourself by believing the vile vomit spewed forth about you by your bully. That is their false opinion of you. That should never be how you think about yourself.

If you find yourself believing their lies, you need to adjust your unproductive thinking.

You are wonderfully and skillfully made. There is no one else out there in the world like you. You never need to change anything about yourself to please a bully or someone else, for that matter. You make changes for you. You oversee you. No one else.

The next time a bully strikes out at you, remember they are hurting inside. They are only trying to hurt you to help them feel better about themselves. It is their twisted way of dealing with pain. It does not make it right. This type of cruel behavior is completely unacceptable. But, understanding why they do it will hopefully help you not take what they have to say to heart.

When you forgive the unforgiveable, you're free.

hurt feelings

If you are feeling hurt because of something mean someone said, what can you do about it?

one:
You can try and talk to the person who hurt you.

warning: If the person who hurt you is a bully, ideas *'two'* or *'three'* might be better options for you to take.

Bullies do not care if they hurt you. That is the reason why they bully you. To hurt you because they are hurting and need to deflect their pain to not feel it themselves.

two:
Pretend the person who hurt you is looking back at you in the mirror. Tell your feelings to your reflection. By doing this exercise, it does not mean you are talking to yourself. Your reflection is standing in proxy for the person who hurt you because you are unable to talk to them directly. You can do this same exercise and talk to yourself.

"Why should I talk to myself? I did not hurt my own feelings."

Maybe you have and never realized it. Maybe you called yourself hurtful names or you did something harmful to yourself physically that you now feel bad about. Sometimes we are cruel to ourselves out of frustration because someone has been hurtful to us. We unconsciously or sometimes consciously turn on ourselves. It is okay to apologize to yourself. It is healing.

three:
Write your feelings down on a piece of paper and then tear it up afterwards.

four:
Tell your feelings to a stuffed animal. Sounds silly, but getting those hurtful feelings out is relieving.

Do not allow yourself to stew over it. Stewing only makes the issue feel worse. It solves nothing.

The sooner you talk about your feelings – no matter what they are - the better you will begin to feel.

Know who you are as a person. That's what matters!

Andy Biersack from the band, *"The Black Veil Brides"* once said, *"As long as you know who you are as a person, nothing else in the world matters."*

What you think of yourself is more important than what others think of you.

Unfortunately, there will always be someone who does not like you no matter what you do, say, wear, eat, where you live, work or who you choose to love. You can run yourself into the ground from exhaustion seeking an unattainable acceptance.

Ask yourself, *"Why do I need this person's approval of me?"*

"Who gave this person whose approval you seek charge of what is and is not acceptable?"

The answer might surprise you. But, you are the one who did.

You may ask, *"How did I do that?"*

Simple. Once you began devaluing yourself based on someone's refusal to give you their approval. No one should ever have that much power over you and your life.

Just because someone cannot see how wonderful you are does not mean you must stop seeing yourself as being wonderful. You are wonderful.

You have the option of choosing to accept their point of view about you or not. Rejection works both ways. You can just as easily reject their negativity about you, as they have rejected you. It honestly is your choice how you choose to see yourself.

The time has come to begin making positive changes in your life. If, that is what you choose. Again, almost everything in life boils down to choices.

Keep in mind, nothing happens overnight. That type of *'false reality'* exists only in television and movies. Real life issues take work. But, start somewhere.

Work on seeing yourself in a positive light, not the darkness you have been standing in because of a bully.

Light or dark.
Free or held captive.
The choice is yours.

fighting a bully battle

The first rule of any battle is - know your enemy.

Although you may never learn the reason why a bully chose you. Just know they are the one with the problem. Not you.

"But, why are they picking on me?" you ask.

The answer may never be known. It doesn't mean there is something wrong with you. There is something wrong within them and they are taking it out on you for some reason only they know why.

A bully lacks the ability to feel compassion or care for another. Their empathy button is broken. They do not care if you cry or kill yourself because of things they did to you. They do not express remorse or regret. They seek pleasure from destroying you. Maintain your power by not showing them they are getting to you – if they are.

"Did you know bullying is just a pathetic ploy a bully uses to keep from dealing with their own issues and pain?"

Until a bully can resolve what is wrong within themselves it is unrealistic to assume they will feel any remorse for their actions towards you. They will continue to gain pleasure from your pain.

The good news is **you can defeat a bully**. And it is easier than you think.

first, get some confidence in yourself.

second, no one is perfect.

Everyone has faults and shortcomings. But, those faults and shortcomings should never be used as ammunition to fight a bully. Pointing out what is wrong with someone makes you a bully, too. Don't do it.

third, stop being so hard on yourself for mistakes or things you may have done that you wish you hadn't.

Those things are over, done with and gone. You cannot go back and undo them. If they were recorded, again, you cannot undo it. The only choice you have is to learn not to do it again. One bad moment, one poor decision in life, does not define who you are. Nor, should it make you feel bad about yourself.

fourth, control is a bully's secret weapon.

Without control, there is no one to put down, belittle or beat-up to help make them feel better about themselves.

Did you get that?

they pick on you to feel better about themselves!

Life is full of battles and obstacles. Anyone who says life is perfect is full of crap. We all go through stuff. Some go through more than others. Those who do, will be stronger in the end if they keep moving forward.

Learn to overcome bullying now and you are well on your way to becoming a Five Star General in the bully battles of life.

Bullying does not end when you graduate high school. But, do not let that scare you. Learn how to defeat bullies now and you will succeed at doing so in your adult life. The only difference is, by then, you will be a much stronger and wiser person.

Strong enough to endure the crap. And wise enough to know how to stop it before it destroys you.

Do not be surprised if you end up helping others learn how to fight and win the bully battle, too. The sharing of knowledge is one of the most precious gifts you can give to another person who is being bullied.

Life is more than whispers in the halls, rumors, the passing around of sexted pictures and videos, bumps, bruises, etc. Please do not give up. Please. Your life has meaning and purpose.

Many schools have put bullying programs in place that offer various suggestions on how to handle bullying. Make sure to check your school for those programs.

how to beat a bully at their own game

"How do I defeat a bully?"

Take control of your life. You do not have to announce it. The result will show when you no longer react to what the bully says or does to you. Not reacting is the worst thing you can do to a bully. To them, it means they have failed and you have successfully stripped their power over you.

Would you like to be my buddy?

Find one person you can befriend in your neighborhood, at school or at church. But, use caution. Keep your guard up. Do not share any secrets about yourself unless that person has truly earned your trust. Protect yourself.

If you have a friend or two who have earned your trust, try and hang out together, especially if you are getting physically attacked by a bully. Being in a small group should help prevent those attacks from happening. There is strength in numbers.

Did you know bully spies exist?

A bully spy is usually tight with a bully. If someone who never paid you any attention, that you know is friends with the bully, suddenly pretends to be enemies with the bully and now wants to be your friend, beware.

Watch what you say and do around a potential bully spy.
Keep them on a *"need to know"* basis. Many have fallen victim to this trick. Do not beat yourself up if you get tricked. They are called spies because they are good at blending in and faking

people out. Anyone can become a victim to this trick, especially someone who has been bullied.

How do I avoid a bully?

When a bully comes towards you, walk in the opposite direction. This does not make you a coward. YOU are the one choosing to walk away. The bully is not making you. You are taking control away from the bully.

Do I get mad or even with a bully?

Neither.

Even if you happen to beat up the bully, do not believe for one minute you won. The bully will try something else to even the score. Many have been fooled into believing after a fist fight, where they kicked the crap out of their bully, that they and the bully could become friends.

In almost every one of those cases, the bully got even.
How? The cruelest way possible. They pretended to be their victim's friend, and, like a venomous snake, struck when their target was at their weakest and most vulnerable state. Beware what you share.

What about giving a bully a taste of their own medicine?

Physical violence and name calling only amps up the tension already brewing between a bully and their victim. Avoid doing it, if possible.
Very rarely does a bully see what a jerk they are. A victim tends to hope down inside a bully will see the error of their ways and stop. But, the truth is although a bully may recognize their own

issues, they either do not care or are afraid to make positive changes.

There are some cases where a bully expressed remorse after their victim died. Some bullies joined up with the parents of the victim to help put a stop to bullying.

"What if I just kill myself? That will show them"

That way of thinking is a complete load of crap. You do not show anyone anything by ending your life because someone decided to treat you horribly. Your death will prove one thing to a bully. The had complete control over you. NEVER give a bully that kind of power over your life!

All your death will succeed in accomplishing is putting your family and friends in an immeasurable amount of unnecessary pain. Before long, classmates will forget about you, graduate and move on with their lives. Meanwhile you will be getting eaten by worms or resting on your parent's mantle in a jar. The bully graduates with a diploma and you get an obituary notice in the paper.

your existence above ground, not your demise underground, is the best revenge to level against your bully. it means you are a survivor – because you are.

So, how do I get the bullying to stop?

ignore the bully. Ignoring a bully is the ultimate up yours. Ignore the bully and you take their power away. It is one of the best moves you can ever make for your own self-preservation. Don't smirk, smile or look pissed off while doing it. Do those things, and the bully knows they can still get to you. Go on with your life as if the bully no longer exists.

If the bully steps into your path, politely ask them to *"Please step out of my way."* If they refuse, do not try and push past them. That is what they want you to do. Instead, turn and walk away. You are not being a chicken. You are taking control of the situation and handling it like a mature person.

tell a trusted adult you are being bullied. It is not uncool to do so.
Nine times out of ten these are people who may have been through it, too, and can provide useful advice on how to handle the situation. Telling an adult, you are being bullied does not make you a snitch, tattle tale or any other childish name.

Telling an adult about a bully, especially a bully who is inflicting physical harm to you or causing you to want to inflict physical harm upon yourself makes you smart! So, do not be afraid to tell.

leave your stuff at home. Whatever the bully wants to take from you, like your IPOD for example, do have it on you. If you do not have your IPOD on you, then the bully cannot take it from you. Does it suck to not be able to have your cool gadgets with you like everyone else around you? Yes. But it is a temporary situation. The bully will eventually understand you have chosen to no longer take their crap and move on.

stop giving the bully ammunition to use against you. Watch what you post online or text on your phone. Keep your private life, private. Try and stay off the Internet as much as possible. *"If you don't have something positive to say, keep your mouth shut and your fingers to yourself."*

take a social media vacation. This will help reduce the stress in your life because you will not be subjected to any negative stuff being said about you. Stop reading the negative things written about you on social media. Shut down your social pages if necessary. Use the block option, too. Avoid sites where you know people are writing mean stuff about you. It is pointless to upset yourself over what trolls write. You will exhaust yourself trying to defend yourself against people who take pleasure in your pain.

So, what if they say stuff about you? So, what! You know the truth and that is all that matters. You do not have to prove anything to anyone. You do not owe them any explanation about your life and your choices.

Believe it or not, years from now all the negative stuff being said about you won't mean a thing to those saying it. Hard to imagine, but it is the truth. Trolls have very short memories. They move from target to target. A year from now, they will be attacking someone else and you will be off their radar.

Are you beginning to understand now how small-minded bullies are?

a time-sucking vampire bully

Do you realize how much of your valuable time is wasted caring about a bully's opinion of you?

Do you realize the bully is literally draining the life out of you like a time-sucking vampire?

Holy Water. A Cross. A Wooden Stake. Sunlight. None of those will help rid you of a TSV Bully. Well, perhaps a bit of garlic breath might keep a bully away for a bit. But, when the garlic disappears, and the bully reappears, then what?

"How do I get rid of a TSV Bully?"

Stop allowing the bully to rob you of your precious time.
Your life matters. Your time matters. And it should not be wasted on a minion who thinks so little of you.

Unlike most Hollywood Vampires, there is nothing mysterious, sexy or cool about a TSV Bully. In fact, they are the reason why many wonderful people end up lying inside of a coffin – having committed suicide.

A victim of a TSV Bully has a right to live their life in peace without being judged for who they are: *gay, straight, bi-sexual, tall, short, skinny, fat, ugly, pretty, smart, dumb, etc...*
Only, the TSV Bully makes sure they don't know it.

Consider a TSV Bully to be a master of illusion. Much like an actual vampire, they cannot see their own reflection. So, instead, they deflect what they know to be the truth about themselves onto others.

"How much time and energy do you spend focused on the way a bully makes you feel about yourself?"

Is it from the moment you wake up until at night when you put your head down on your pillow to sleep? And, even then, the pain you feel because of their behavior is managing to turn pleasant dreams into nightmares.

You probably go through a dozen wardrobe changes, hairstyles, make-up applications, and such, before heading off to school.

"Do you realize you are doing those things for a bully and not yourself?"

A TSV Bully will never be won over, so stop spinning your wheels and trying to be perfect for their approval. Perfection is not only overrated, it is impossible to achieve, especially with a TSV Bully.

Take a moment and ask yourself, *"Why do I care what a TSV Bully thinks of me?"*

Hasn't this TSV Bully stolen enough from you already?

There is no pleasing a selfish, immature, misguided person with issues that can only be resolved once they realize that:

1. They have a problem.
2. They want to fix the problem.
3. They are sincere in wanting to change their mean ways.

A bully will continue being a bully until they fix what is broken from within. There is nothing you, nor anyone else, can say or do that will change their behavior.

A bully has the power of choice, same as you. They can choose to change their life and get help, or they can choose to remain in pain and continue tormenting others to help them alleviate it.

If a bully chooses the later, it does not mean you must remain in misery. Their choice does not have to be your choice, too. You can choose to act and take your life back.

question:

"Who can be a Time-Sucking Vampire Bully?"

answer:

Any person who willfully, maliciously and deliberately chooses to steal time away from another person's life by methods of distraction such as; calling them mean names, spreading rumors and/or inflicting physical harm.

Ask yourself, *"Who allowed a TSV Bully control over my life?"*

This question has a two-part answer.

first, you are to blame.

"How am I to blame? I'm the victim."

A TSV Bully got a hook into you, once you allowed what they said and/or did to you, to steal the joy from your life and focus all your attention, time and feelings on them. Please understand, this is not your fault. Believe it or not, this is the way most people respond when attacked. It's normal, until you gain better knowledge on your enemy.

You need to realize that you are the one who oversees your life. You are the one who determines what you will/will not accept in your life.

"Are you going to continue allowing a TSV Bully control to have control over your life?"

Look at your experience with a TSV Bully as a wake-up call. Recognize the areas in your life that need work and put your focus on it. By doing so, you will begin developing into a stronger person who is better able to handle issues and not lose their power, again.

No matter what a TSV Bully has said or made you believe about yourself, start accepting yourself, faults and all. Stop feeling bad about yourself just because someone does not like something about you. That is their misfortune, not yours. Never feel like you must change who you are to please someone else.

Everyone is a work in progress with varying issues, even your bully. Scary thought, right? You are not alone. If it means talking to your parents, talk to them. If it means getting professional help, get it. Stop allowing the joy to be robbed from your life, whether it is because of a bully or what they may have stirred up that already existed down inside of you.

You deserve happiness. Question is, do you choose it?

second, a TSV Bully has what you might call *'A God Complex'*. They are a legend in their own mind. They are incapable of seeing the arrogant, pompous, cruel, narcissistic human being they have evolved into because of their own pain.

Yes, you read that last part right. They are hurting, too.
The difference between you and a TSV Bully is, they choose to cause hurt to others to deal with their pain instead of getting help and learning better coping skills.

A TSV Bully is not the boss of you. So, stop taking orders from them. The time has come for you to take a stand for your life. You oversee you - no one else.

Do remember one thing. Your parents have a say over your life until you are 18 years old. Do not forget that. Always respect your parents, even when you disagree with them about something. You may not always listen to what they have to say, (*which is normal*), but respect them always.

Life truly is too short to waste away on a TSV Bully and their negativity. A TSV Bully will not even matter once you graduate and move forward with your life. So, why allow them to matter now?

If you are reading this in the morning, today is a new day.

If you are reading this mid-day or at night, tomorrow is a new day.

Be free. Live your life. You only get one. Make the most of it.

Was a bully the only one who hurt me?

It never feels good to hear someone say to your face;

"You are stupid."

"You are ugly."

"You are a loser."

"You are nothing."

Ask yourself, *"Are the salty tears rolling down my cheeks because of what the bully said to me or, did those hurtful words trigger a hidden pain I never realized existed?"*

If the hurtful words triggered a hidden pain, you may be wondering, *"How did the bully know something was going on inside of me before I did?"*

A bully does not need to know the root of your pain. They sense a weakness in you, and then zero in on it like a heat seeking missile.

In the wild kingdom, it is common for animals to attack a weaker, sicker member of the pack or deliberately isolate them from the group.

True, a bully is not an animal, despite their behavior dictating otherwise. But, like an animal in the wild, they sense weakness and then attack and socially isolate their prey.

Ask yourself the following questions:

"What is the true root of your pain?"

"Did your parents got divorced?"

"Do you lack a close relationship with your Mom/Dad/Sibling(s)?"

"Did you lose someone who you were once close to?"

"Did you lose someone you admired?"

"Did you lose someone who helped you feel good about yourself? If so, do you feel lost without them?"

"Do you not feel good looking enough?"

"Do not think you are smart enough?"

"Are there any family secrets you may have blocked out or are afraid to tell someone about?"

"Do you feel that something might be your fault when it might not be your fault at all?"

Close your eyes and search down in your soul for the honest answer. Only you know what key will open your Pandora's Box. Think.

Do not get frustrated or upset if the answer does not come to you right away. It will, when the time is right. Once you learn the issue, seek help to resolve it, heal from it and then put it behind you.

"How do I do this?"

Talk to your parents, a professional counselor or a trusted adult who can help you take the next step towards healing.

Do not be afraid to put a light on whatever the issue may be and deal with it. Stop letting it torment you and cause you pain and distress. You do not deserve or need to carry it.

No matter your age or how long the issue has been going on, it is never too late to seek help. Why spend your life full of pain when you don't have to? Deal with it and heal from it.

So, are you ready?

The time has come to step boldly towards a new, brighter and happier future.

Stop letting a bully feed on your existing pain like a life-taking, blood-sucking leech. You have the ability and the power to starve them. How? By no longer reacting or responding to their attacks.

Aren't you sick and tired of hurting all the time?

It takes a very brave person to face their demons, no matter what they might be. And you are brave. Whether you realize it now or not.

Being able to sort out your issues is a courageous step towards healing and recovery. Nobody else can get inside of your head and heart and fix things. Only you have the power to make it happen.

Through hard-work and dedication on your part, you will reach a place where you can live a more balanced, productive life and be free from past pains.

Living the perfect life is unrealistic. No one lives a perfect life. No one. If you expect to live a perfect life, you will gain nothing but endless struggles and disappointments.

So, expect to live a life full of ups and downs. By recognizing this realistic fact, you will lead a more balanced life with a solid foundation.

Though you may not forget, you will eventually get to a place where you can forgive. And once you forgive, you are free. You are healed.

franken-bully

If you are a bully, please consider a change in your cruel behavior. Being spiteful and nasty to others is not what your life is supposed to be about. Behaving like a jerk does not make you a better or stronger person. Nor, does it make you a leader worthy of respect or recognition. Acting vile towards someone only reveals you have serious issues in your life that need to be dealt with on a professional level. Know that anyone who teases you for that has now become a bully, too.

There is no shame in wanting, needing and getting help for your issues. It takes a courageous person to acknowledge they have a problem and then take steps towards healing.

"Why go through life being pissed off, hurt and acting mean to people just to help ease your own pain?"

"Why behave this way when you can heal from the pain and live a happier life?"

"Are you ready to make an appointment with Dr. Franken-Bully and stop being a bully?"

new brain:
think before you speak.
think before you act.
think before you react.
think.

new eyes:
to see things differently.
to notice others besides yourself.
to view others in a positive way instead of being so judgmental and critical.
to view yourself in a positive way instead of being so judgmental and critical.

new mouth:
say something nice to someone.
say something nice about someone.
say something nice about yourself.
learn to keep your mouth shut if you cannot say anything nice.

new heart:
feel compassion towards others.
feel empathy towards others.
feel love towards others.
feel love towards yourself.

new hands/arms:
to shake another's hand with.
to write an apology to those whom you have hurt.
to wave "Hello" instead of giving someone the middle finger or punching them.
to give hugs to others.
to give hugs to yourself.
to accept hugs from others.

new legs and feet:
to walk away from a situation before starting anything you will regret.
to walk up to someone whom you have been bullying and say, "I'm sorry."

so, what do you think?

Up until now, you have believed everything a bully said is wrong with you. You've cried, gotten mad, felt frustrated and more. Are you ready to throw their negative opinion of you in the garbage and develop a positive opinion of yourself, for yourself, instead?

"How do I get positive opinions of myself?"

You can start with talking to the important people in your life: Family members, friends, teachers, counselors and your pastor.

Their input might help inspire you to see the positive things in yourself you have been overlooking because of being overly focused on the negative things. Sometimes a little constructive criticism helps open our eyes to that which we are unable to see.

Here are some examples of questions to help get you started:

Listen, it never hurts to ask. You will not know the answer until you do. You can do this. You need to do this to start seeing yourself in a new, more positive light. You need to get control of your life.

What do you think of me?

What do you like about me?

What don't you like about me?

What is your favorite thing about me?

What do you see in me as weaknesses?

What do you see in me as strengths?

If you could improve one thing about me, what would it be?

If you could change one thing about me, what would it be?

If you could leave something about me the same, what would it be?

Constructive criticism should never be viewed as a terrible thing. If what is being said to you is constructive, take it under advisement. If it is destructive, throw it in the trash.

Constructive criticism can sometimes come across harsh. Try not to get defensive or dismissive. Keep an open-mind. Take the time to think over what was said. The constructive words may not be what you want to hear, but they might be what you need to hear to become a better, stronger person.

coffin-quences

Dear Bully,

Why are you choosing to act mean towards others?

Does it make you feel better about yourself when you put another person down?

Do you feel like an important person while acting like a bully?

Do you feel special? Needed? Accepted by others when behaving like a bully?

Do you lack the ability to have control your own life so, you must control other people's lives?

Do you even recognize how your cruel actions towards another cause devastating consequences, some that last a lifetime?

Do you even realize how your vile and vicious actions towards another might cause them to end their life?

Do you even care?

While **legally** bullying someone to death does not make you a murderer - **technically** it does.

True, people are responsible for the choices they make. And if a person chooses to end their life, that is their choice.

But, what if your cruel behavior towards the person, forced the person to make a choice they might not have otherwise made without your cruel influence? Can you see the possibility of that happening? All behaviors, right or wrong, have consequences.

If you bullied someone and they ended their life, **YOU made them CHOOSE** that harsh solution to their pain based on your selfish, relentless, cruelty, just to relieve your own pain.

"Who put you in charge of deciding who has the right to be left alone and who has the right to be bullied, sometimes to the point of committing suicide because of it?"

To those who bully others, take this under advisement and consideration for which is intended:

'Just because you choose to behave in a vindictive, cruel manner does not make it acceptable behavior: socially, morally, or ethically.'

You have no right to mistreat another person for your own personal amusement. You are making a choice to behave this way.

You have no right to mistreat another person to help relieve your own pain. Get professional help. Grow-up. You are making a choice to behave this way.

You have no right to tear someone down in the hopes of building yourself up. You are making a choice to behave this way.

It is never too late to correct unacceptable behavior. Are you ready to stop being a bully? If your answer is "No!", you had better hit your knees and start praying for mercy, because you are going to need it for the rest of your sad, hate-fueled, miserable, empty life. Do you honestly want to live your life feeling that way?

Ask yourself these questions and really take some time to think about your answer:

"What has got you so upset down inside that you feel the need to strike out at people?"

"What do you really get out of behaving like a bully towards others?"

"Does acting like a bully make you feel good about yourself?"

"Do you feel bad about yourself when you bully someone?"

"Do you feel like you are accomplishing something when acting like a bully?"

"Did someone teach you how to be a bully? If so, who? Why?"

"Do you have any self-respect?"

"Why are you so full of hate and anger towards the person whom you bully?"

"Do they remind you of the person you wish to be, but can't?"

"Are you jealous of them?"

"Do you envy something they have?"

"Why are you behaving like a bully?"

Have you ever heard the saying, *"You catch more flies with honey than with vinegar?"*

Being nasty to others gets you nowhere in life. You might feel big, tough and mighty, pushing your weaker peers around, but, you are acting like a small-minded fool.

If you do not get to the root of what is really eating at your soul you will wind up leading a very shallow, empty, meaningless, cold, hard life. No joy. No peace. No true happiness. Nothing.

On the surface, you may appear to have everything. But, deep down inside where you really live, you will be empty.

Now, ask yourself the same questions asked of those whom you have bullied:

"What is the root of your pain? Your anger? Your self-loathing?"

"Did your parents got divorced?"

"Do you lack a close relationship with your Mom/Dad/Sibling(s)?"

"Did you lose someone who you were once close to?"

"Did you lose someone you admired?"

"Did you lose someone who helped you feel good about yourself? If so, do you feel lost without them?"

"Do you not feel good looking enough?"

"Do not think you are smart enough?"

"Are there any family secrets you may have blocked out or are afraid to tell someone about?"

"Do you feel that something might be your fault when it might not be your fault at all?"

Close your eyes and search down in your soul for the honest answer. Only you know what key will open your Pandora's Box. Think.

Do not get frustrated or upset if the answer does not come to you right away. It will, when the time is right. Once you learn the issue, seek help to resolve it, heal from it and then put it behind you.

Right now, you are viewed as the enemy.

But, much like those whom you have picked on and put down, you too can change your situation around. You can choose to stop being the bad guy. The bully.

You can choose to live a life of happiness instead of anger. If you do decide to shed your evil ways, it will not make you a punk, a wussy or a sell-out. You will be a mature person who is trying to make changes for the better.

Through hard-work and an honest effort, you can become a person who will earn the right kind of respect, instead of demanding what you thought was respect from others, but was, fear.

Being mean to others is not respectful. It is disrespectful.

If you grew up in a household where you were taught to handle issues by being physically/mentally/ emotionally cruel to others, it does not mean you must continue the cycle of abuse. That is what you have endured. Abuse.

If you continue to willfully behave like a bully, you will eventually be held accountable for your actions. It might not be today. It might not be tomorrow. But, it will happen.

It is inexcusable, unacceptable behavior to hound somebody day after day until they cannot take it anymore and are forced to do something drastic to stop it – like committing suicide.

"How would you feel if the shoe were on the other foot?"

Take a moment and step into your victim's shoes.

"How would you feel receiving harassing phone calls, to be beaten up daily, to have people throw water bottles and trash at you, to have rumors posted about you on social media?"

It is so pointless to be at odds with someone you hardly know over nothing, or perhaps something that will not even matter a year or two from now. Grow-up. Choose a better path. Stop making people hurt so you do not have to hurt. It is cruel, childish and selfish.

If you choose to screw your life up, fine. That is your choice. But, you do not have the right to screw someone else's life up in the process.

The time has come to work towards making positive changes and becoming a better person, not only for you, but for those around you, too.

You need to let that better person, the one who has been living inside of you since birth, the one who has been smothered by the angry, hurtful person you have had on display, free.

Are you ready to make a change?

signs i'm being bullied

I cannot sleep well.
I have bruises and cuts that I hide.
I cry for no reason.
I make up excuses like I am sick, so I don't have to go to school.
I do not want to eat.
I feel sad.
I am moody.
I get called mean names.
Nobody wants to by my friend.
I want to go to sleep and never wake up.

if you are feeling suicidal or having bad thoughts of any kind, please do the following right away:

***Tell your parents**
***Call a Suicide Prevention Hotline**
***Call 911**
***Talk to your teacher, your counselor, your principal**
***Talk to your pastor**
***Contact a Bully Prevention Organization**
***Talk to a responsible adult**

There is nothing to feel embarrassed or ashamed about when asking for help.

UNDER NO CIRCUMSTANCES SHOULD YOU END YOUR LIFE. Ending your life is not like a video game. You cannot hit the *"start over"* button if you change your mind and decide to live after you are already dead. Get it? Got it? Good.

how to heal from being bullied

first.
Turn it over to God.

Before you get all self-righteous, let me point out something. This is not a religious matter. This is more:

"Hey, I'm tired of carrying the burden. Here, God, you take it for a while. I need a break."

Giving your problems over to God is a way of letting go. It begins the healing process and helps ease the burden off you. You have been carrying undeserving and unnecessary garbage long enough. Wouldn't you agree? So, hand it over.

second.
Forgive the person(s) who did you wrong. This does not require you to say it to their face(s). In fact, you can think it in your head, feel it in your heart, write it down on paper for your eyes only and then tear it up or tell it to your stuffed animals.

Ask yourself, *"Do I want to give a bully power over me to the point where I spend the rest of my life bitter and angry because of what they did to me?"* If you want to be free from it, your answer should be *"No!"*

Carrying bitterness and anger is not worth the long-term damage it will do to you physically, mentally and emotionally. A bully is not worth it. It has even been proven that sickness can develop from unresolved anger. Forgive them and move on.

third.

Forgive yourself. You are not to blame for being bullied. The bullying you received or have been receiving was probably done through no fault of your own. But, it has left you feeling bad about yourself, mad, confused, depressed and who knows what else.

The important thing to note is you have eyes now to see what went wrong. So, forgive yourself for being lost for a while.

The healing process can now begin.

hope

bad days 50%
good days 50%

a splash in the rain

instead of wishing the rain away

this time i think i'll go out and play

as grown-ups, under the covers we huddle

As kids, we jump and splash in the puddles

gene kelly adored, *"singing in the rain"*

an umbrella, a heel kick, a twirl of the cane

earthworms squiggle up from beneath the ground

i stretch forth my arms and spin around

such fun to let your tongue catch the drops

until the sun appears, and the rain finally stops

hence, from now on, if it should rain

instead of complaining of it being a pain

i'm going to head outside through the door

to jump and splash in puddles forevermore.

Who is your best friend?
Who is your worst enemy?
Who gives you love?
Who gives you hate?
Who encourages you?
Who discourages you?
Who believes in you?
Who doubts you?
Who has a gallon of fear?
Who has a pint of faith?
You.

Real courage is bravery
that builds with each challenge.
No one can scare it or chase it away.
Real courage roars when pushed
and purrs when nudged.
Real courage conquers uncertainity
and replaces doubt.
Real courage rids the mind of fear
and replaces it with faith.
Real courage arrives when least expected
and vanishes just as quickly.
Real courage flouishes with each
bold step taken in life.

Self-worth cannot be purchased.
It is not found on a store shelf.
Self-worth is a value that fluctuates in life.
Self-worth prospers with positive words.
Self-worth becomes poor with negative words.
Self-worth conquers weaknesses
and replaces insecurities.
Self-worth replaces misery with contentment.
Self-worth is easy to possess, but just as easy to lose.
Self-worth, although free, can also bear a heavy price when choosing to value yourself.
Self-worth remains if you let it.

Confidence is strength residing from within.
No one can defeat or take it away,
unless you permit it.
Confidence speaks with force and yet,
listens with a tender ear.
Confidence overcomes fear.
Confidence crushes barriers
and opens roads and doors.
Confidence demands respect, but not arrogance.
Confidence aides your future with each step taken.

The circumstance is always subject to change.

You don't have to fit in.
It's good to stand out.

Be yourself! If someone does not like you for who you are that is their problem, not yours. Aren't you exhausted from being a people pleaser hoping to win someone's approval?

Each snowflake is unique just like you. There is no one else on earth who can be you, except YOU. Be yourself.

Curiosity killed the cat!

Ur NOT a cat!

Deactivate Ur Social Networking Accounts!
Don't Peek!
Don't Go Back!
Block The Drama!
Delete Negative Stuff From Ur Life
And U Defeat The Bully!
Disconnect Social Media –
Reconnect w/Life!

One step at a time defeats a bully

"Which step are you standing on in the bully battle you have been fighting?"

The 'I can't' step or the 'I can' step?

"Are you ready to stop allowing a bully to have control over your life and dictate how you should feel about yourself?"

If so, you just took the first step. *"Congratulations!"*

No one recalls what we were like at birth. We don't remember how all we could do was lay wherever Mom or Dad put us. We soon learned to roll over and, eventually crawl. And, after some trial and error, we mastered walking one wobbly step at a time.

The point is, you may stumble. You may even wobble and fall over. But, the key is to get back up, dust yourself off and try again.

If you want to succeed in life, you need to keep on climbing the steps and never let anyone or anything stand in your way.

Success is not measured by popularity, money in the bank or a job title. Success is trying – even if you fail. At least, you tried. And that, is more than most people do.

Speak outward and you will be heard.
Continue speaking inward and you won't.

Sometimes we really need to talk to someone.
Sometimes we really should talk to someone.

But, how do you talk to someone?
What do you say?
How do you start?

Are you afraid what you want to say might come out wrong?

Are you worried that if you talk to someone they will even hear what you are saying or truly get how you feel?

The only way you'll ever know is to speak. Talk to a trusted adult: a Parent, an Aunt or Uncle, your School Counselor, a Police Officer, a Fireman, or a Teacher.

Nothing in your life will change until you speak up and let someone know you are hurting.

H8ters are gonna h8te
Playas are gonna play
Bullies are gonna bully
I'm gonna stay.

Don't kill yourself.
Will yourself to live.

The bully can get to know my back side, as I walk away from their hateful crap.

Shut the F-Up
I don't care what you have to say
Shut the F-Up
Leave me alone, just go away

You pretend to be my friend
You pretend to care
Shut the F-Up
And get rid of that shocked stare

Shut the F-Up
I'm so onto your tricks and lies
I know exactly who you turned into your little bully spy

Shut the F-up
You'll cause me to hurt no longer
Shut the F-up
Yup, that's right, I'm getting stronger

Shut the F-Up
For it's my turn to speak
I said Shut the F-Up
You're the one who is pathetic
The one who's weak

Shut the F-Up
I'll never be heartless like you
Shut the F-Up
I've spoken my peace
You can leave...we're through

Shut the F-Up
I refuse to end my life
I refuse to let you win
I refuse to be consumed with strife

Shut the F-up
I'm a winner
A life chooser
Shut the F-Up
You sorry, little Bully loser.

Cutting causes pain
Cut downs gnaw at my brain
I wish your slander out of my head
Before I wind up lost and dead.

Call me what you want
My guts I refuse to spill
You cannot break my spirit
Or rob me of my will.

Go look in a mirror and say all that bad sh** you say about me to yourself. I realize now you are really talking about yourself.

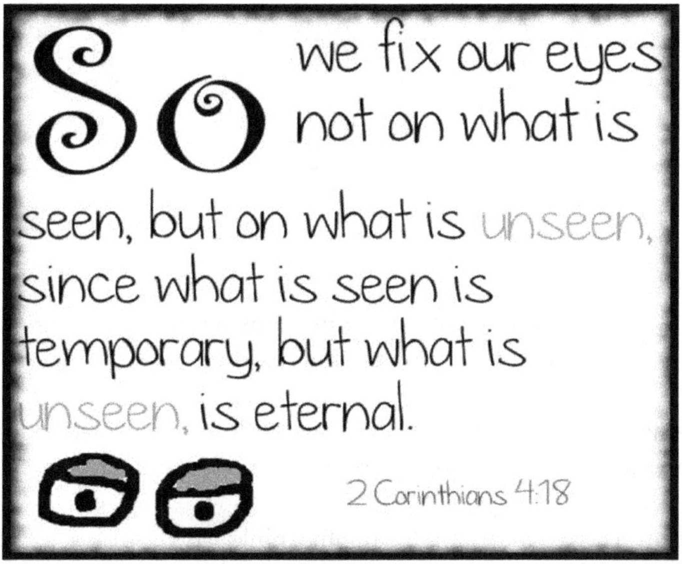

So we fix our eyes not on what is
seen, but on what is unseen,
since what is seen is
temporary, but what is
unseen, is eternal.
2 Corinthians 4:18

Isn't it ironic
Being a bully made you iconic
Having people live in fear
Afraid of their reputation being smeared

Wish everyone had eyes to see
The pleasure you take in causing their misery
Shallow and weak is what you are
With a heart coated in painful, hidden scars

I long for the day bullies get taken down
I long for the day they are run out of town
Then their bullied victims will finally be free
To be who they are and live a life full of glee.

Did you know salmon swim upstream, enduring and overcoming countless obstacles along the way?

Weak salmon cannot take the ups and downs of the journey and quit. Strong salmon overcome the odds and thrive.

Contrary to what a bully might think, you are not a weak salmon. You are a strong salmon, capable of metaphorically swimming against rushing currents, leaping over large rocks and escaping the fierce clutches of your enemies.

Life will toss obstacles into your path to make things difficult. Like a bully, for example: who will call you mean names, spread rumors about you or physically assault you.

No matter what is tossed into your path, remember, you are a strong salmon. Strong salmon do not quit! Strong salmon continue swimming forward, leaving obstacles, hidden in a flurry of bubbles stirred up by their tail fin.

To quote *Dory* from the movie, *Finding Nemo*, "*Just Keep Swimming*" no matter what obstacles are put into your path.

End the pain. Start talking.

"Hi!" friend
"Bye!" friend
Did you know I'm bringing my life to an end?

Of course, you don't
You never had the time
Always mistaken me for a pathetic mime

I pass you daily in the hall
I listen carefully
But my name you never called

I needed a good friend
Not a *"Hi"* and *"Bye"* friend
Someone to be an actual friend

I'm tired of being picked on
Being alone and treated like crap
So tired, am I, of the daily fighting
My zest for life is zapped

Every night before I go to sleep
I pray to the Lord my soul to keep
And if He should be able to work it in
I hope you and I will become real friends.

i will not put myself down.

i will use my mind and not my hands if an unpleasant situation happens.

i will not sext.

i will appreciate the body I was given.

i will work hard for what I want.

i will accomplish all my goals.

i will not compliment myself too much, nor put myself down.

i will have patience when I am in a hurry.

i will not argue with my parents.

i will be faithful in my choices.

i will not envy others for the things they have.

i will trust myself.

i will not be cruel to someone who has been cruel to me.

i will lose my heart to someone.

i will remember that I don't have it that bad, but only when I think that I do.

i will love myself even if I don't feel like it.

i will dig deep inside for strength when I feel that I am weak.

i will respect my parents/guardian/foster.

i will learn right from wrong.

i will use manners when eating with a poor man and practice the same manners with a rich man.

i will not be greedy.

i will not destroy my body. I will respect it and expect others to do the same.

i will deactivate my social media accounts for a month and see if helps me feel better.

i will stick up for someone who is being bullied.

i will not bully anyone for any reason.

I have rights.
I have the right not to be hit.
I have the right not to be called mean names.
I have the right not to be judged.
I have the right to defend myself.
I have the right to be left alone.
I have the right to exist.

Here is a little secret: "*Bullies are unhappy with themselves. It is the reason why they hurt you.*"

You hate my face
I hate yours more
Do me a favor
And hit the door!

I'm sick of your ranting
Your teasing and lies
I'm especially sick
Of your internet spies

Crawl back under the rock
From whence you came
If the truth were known
You're the one who is lame

But, you keep on bullying me
While in the past that used to work
You no longer have power over me
You are a pathetic lost jerk.

Block. Delete. And, you defeat cyberbullying.

a bully's bubble
is only as strong as the air
you allow the bully to blow
into it!

A bad moment in life does not define who you are.

Never say something to someone you would not want said to you.

Love is always stronger than hate.

If opossums could speak, they would understand how it feels to have lies spread about you.

People tell lies about opossums all the time. Most are borne out of ignorance, much like a bully does to their victim.

Opossums are judged by their appearance, what they eat, for playing dead *(a defense mechanism against predators)* and for hanging upside down *(a myth).*

The truth about opossums: they *"play dead"* or go into a catatonic state to avoid danger, they hiss and show their teeth to scare you away, they only bite if you try to pick them up, they carry fewer diseases than cats and dogs, they are very clean, despite stinking sometimes if they rummaged through trash looking for food, they are immune to most snake venom, they have opposable thumbs on their rear feet and, their fur feels kind of like a stuffed animal.

Despite those confirmed facts, it is difficult convincing people to see them any other way besides, dirty, nasty and diseased – per the misinformed lies or rumors.

But, circumstances are subject to change for the opossum, and you, too.

Thanks to Dr. Claire Komives with the *San José State University*, things for opossums are about to change. Dr. Komives is currently working on developing an opossum-based snake bite antidote that could one day save a human from a venomous snake bite. Amazing, right?

Just like there is wonder in an opossum yet to be realized, there is wonder yet to be realized in you, too.

Although you may never convince a bully or anyone who believes the lies the bully spread otherwise, you know the truth. And, believe it or not, that is what matters.

Sometimes ignorance cannot be overcome. But, that is okay. Those who are worthy of your time will not listen to the lies. Those who do? Forget them. They are not worth anymore of your valuable time.

Vicious rumors and lies never stopped an opossum from living its life. Why let the lies and rumors stop you?

It's *im-possum-able* to please everyone. Stop exhausting yourself trying.

You say you're not mean
I don't know what you mean
Because your actions towards me
Don't justify the means
Why are you so mean?
Do you know what I mean?
I don't think you have the brains to get what I mean
But, I get what you mean
I do understand what you mean
The fact is, you are plain mean.

The bully waits patiently to cast their hex
Reading everything you post on-line or in a text

The bully comes disguised as a friend, but is a foe
Never trust someone you do not really know

Beware of what you post on-line or in a text
It lives forever passing from one bully to the next.

Bullies hate themselves more than they hate those whom they pick on.

Better to be unpopular than be a bully. It is not worth treating others poorly to feel better about yourself.

Bullies have issues.
I can see that now.
I may not be perfect.
But, I am finally free.
I know now who you really are.
Yet, you still don't know me.

If you cannot accept the way you look, then why should you expect others to do the same? Accept yourself.

Sometimes a good cry helps release the pain.

It is okay to love yourself.

You do not deserve to be bullied.

Your future is waiting. But, you must be here to live it.

It is not the garbage a bully says or writes about you. It is how you receive it. Garbage comes in. Garbage goes out.

Everyone is beautifully flawed.

Accept what you can change.
Let go of what you cannot change.

You have the power to choose.

A bully sees flaws because they are flawed.
You see character because you are real.

You do not need someone to make you happy. Be happy with yourself, first.

An internet bully is just a lost soul trapped inside the body of a heartless troll.

Be yourself.

When a bully talks you walk away.

Shove me?
I will not shove you back.

Steal my laptop?
I will use pen and paper.

Take my iPod?
I will whistle instead.

Write nasty things on my locker?
I will paint it.

Try and start a fight?
I will ignore you.

I'm sick of your demented games.
You, bullying me, has become really lame.

I will stand up.
I will speak out.
I will help a kid who is being bullied.
If I don't, then I am saying *"It is okay to bully"*.
And it is not okay to bully.

Lips may flap, words may fly.
I know the truth and can hold my head high.
It does not matter what I have done or said.
Facing my bully, I now no longer dread.

If you do not want it spoken about you, do not speak it about someone else.

Though I may be in pain, I refuse to die in vain. Bullying is not worth ending my life over.

I am not nothing.
I am something.
I am not nobody.
I am somebody.

God does not make mistakes.

Live in peace. Do not rest in peace.

Respect yourself.

It is okay to feel mad sometimes.
It is okay to feel sad sometimes.
It is not okay to feel mad and sad all the time.

90% of what you feel is all about your mental attitude. Keep it positive.

Every day is a choice.

Speak pleasant things over yourself or *"Shh!"*

The bullied do not always become the bully.

Learn from it.
Move on.
Don't repeat it.

Being bullied is not your fault.

You have strength to survive. Draw on it. You got this!

I have no friends.
I have no money.
All I have is rumors, bruises, heartbreak and pain.

I do have one thing.

I have God.
He's on my side.
He'll never betray me.
He'll never lie to me.
He'll never use me.
He'll never smack me.
He'll never steal from me.
He'll see me through this time in my life.
He'll always stand beside me and be my friend no matter what others say or do to me.

My life might not mean much to you.
But, it means something to me.
I refuse to allow a bully take that away from me.

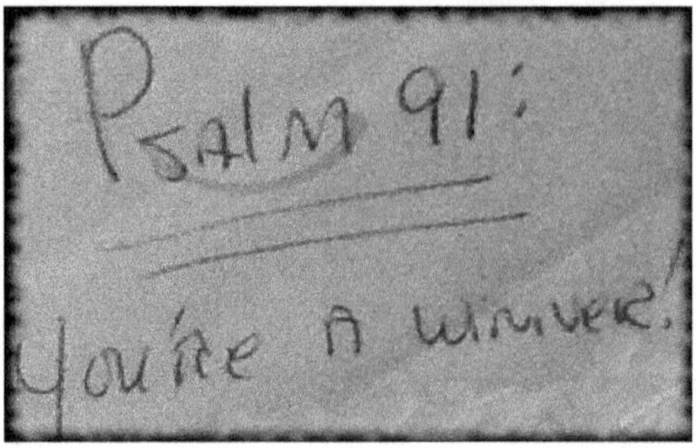

PSALM 91

© Amplified Bible/Lockman Foundation

1 He who dwells in the secret place of the Most High shall remain stable and fixed under the shadow of the Almighty [Whose power no foe can withstand].

2 I will say of the Lord, He is my Refuge and my Fortress, my God; on Him I lean and rely, and in Him I [confidently] trust!

3 For [then] He will deliver you from the snare of the fowler and from the deadly pestilence.

4 [Then] He will cover you with His pinions, and under His wings shall you trust and find refuge; His truth and His faithfulness are a shield and a buckler.

5 You shall not be afraid of the terror of the night, nor of the arrow (the evil plots and slanders of the wicked) that flies by day,

6 Nor of the pestilence that stalks in darkness, nor of the destruction and sudden death that surprise and lay waste at noonday.

7 A thousand may fall at your side, and ten thousand at your right hand, but it shall not come near you.

8 Only a spectator shall you be [yourself inaccessible in the secret place of the Most High] as you witness the reward of the wicked.

9 Because you have made the Lord your refuge, and the Most High your dwelling place,

10 There shall no evil befall you, nor any plague or calamity come near your tent.

11 For He will give His angels [especial] charge over you to accompany and defend and preserve you in all your ways [of obedience and service].

12 They shall bear you up on their hands, lest you dash your foot against a stone.

13 You shall tread upon the lion and adder; the young lion and the serpent shall you trample underfoot.

14 Because he has set his love upon Me, therefore will I deliver him; I will set him on high, because he knows and understands My name [has a personal knowledge of My mercy, love, and kindness—trusts and relies on Me, knowing I will never forsake him, no, never].

15 He shall call upon Me, and I will answer him; I will be with him in trouble, I will deliver him and honor him.

16 With long life will I satisfy him and show him My salvation.

Before you were born, God had already created you to be someone very special. You have a great purpose, worth and value in this life. Do not listen to the haters. Trust what God said. He's been here longer.

Please, stay.

You have a voice. Use it. Speak up.

Was once introverted because of a bully.
Now I'm extroverted because of courage.

Why does a bully, bully?
Because they are hurting.
Because they are insecure.
Because they need to feel better about themselves.
Because they want attention.
Because they seek approval.
Because they think they are cool.

You can handle life.

Delete accounts.
Unfriend foes.
Liberate yourself.

Be a Prince
Don't react and be mean
People will adore you
The bully now bows to the new King.

Stupid Geek Mistake ?
UR ATTENTION SEEKING
Fag Moron Emo
LAME :)~
HARSH Weirdo Slut
Nerd WORDS Pig
Dumb Ass
DO
Freak X Muffin Top
NOT
MATTER
Skank Poser Idiot
:)~ ANYMORE! MY
Wannabe
Jerk Whale
GO DEAF
WHEN-
EARS Whore Strange
Bitch
EVER Gay U Bimbo
Dumb
UR MOUTH
OPEN Loser
Ugly AND SPEAK! Fat
WHATEVER

You are what a bully says you are, but only if you believe them. So, don't.

If you want to have a good attitude about yourself, you can. If you want to feel sorry for yourself you can do that, too. It is always your choice.

The day a bully no longer controls you, is the day you are free.

Think before you react.

I will still be standing when you fall. And you will fall.
All bullies do.

Bullies enjoy calling their victims hurtful words. But, what do the words a bullied victim gets called really mean?

Let's look at some words bullies say:

slut:
A person who is sexually promiscuous or has loose sexual morals.

ugly:
Unpleasant or repulsive in appearance.

useless:
A person who has no ability or skill in a specific area or activity.

loser:
A person who is unable to succeed or is incompetent.

Notice how nowhere in any of the definitions above does a name appear. Your name. Once you understand the words a bully says about you, they lose their meaning and power. Why? Because they are untrue and therefore do not matter. Especially coming from the mouth of someone with issues of their own.

words do not define who you are as a person.

Words only have life if you choose to believe them. If you choose to ignore them, they die on the tips of your ears and never to take root in your heart.

Killing yourself doesn't show *"them"*.
Surviving does.

Shut down all social media accounts during a bully attack. If a bully cannot reach you, they cannot hurt you.

Royal bully sitting upon thine throne
Telling the school to ignore me, to leave me alone
Barking orders and acting like you have got class
But, remove the crown and staff you hold
What's left? Nothing but a royal pain in my ass.

My head is held high
My foot is out the door
I am choosing to step into a new life
One where I will not tolerate being bullied anymore.

Feeling wounded
Drowning in dread
A million random thoughts
Circle inside my head

You are better off dead
Is what they speak
Maybe they're right
I am pathetic, I am weak

Am I as bad as they have made me out to be?
Wait! No! I am not!
It is they, who are pathetic
It is they, who are weak

It is easy to deflect
What you'll never be
A caring, loving person
You'll never be like me.

Uncover.
Discover.
Recover.
Live.

What would you do

If I suddenly walked up to you
And ordered you to take that back
Bet you'd launch into a panic attack

Well, what are you waiting for?
Take it back, right this minute
I am not kidding with you
I am serious, I mean it

I dare you to treat me nice
I dare you to be my friend
Aww, what's the matter, bully
You don't know how to pretend?

Relax
I will show you how it is done
You smile for the world
In private you come undone

Punching, screaming, hating
So many feelings, it's overwhelming
Your nose will start to run
Tear stained eyes grow red from the swelling

What's that you say?
You don't have time for this sh**
I should go and do what with myself
Look out! Right hook! Here comes the hit

I finally did what was long overdue
Thought hitting someone is not the right thing to do
But I needed to take control of life back
Not to be vengeful, but to prevent more bully attacks.

Deliberately being cruel to others to feel better about yourself is seriously messed up thinking.

How does someone defeat hurtful feelings and thoughts? With strength from within. It cannot come from anyone else.

The person being bullied needs to realize for themselves they are not the one with the problem and tune out anything the bully says or does.

The person being bullied must make the decision they will no longer rule their mood, feelings, emotions or choices based on what a bully says or does.

The person being bullied needs to know they are not alone when it comes to being bullied. There are many others out there who have been bullied, too.

The person being bullied needs to understand they are not the one who is weak, pathetic, dumb, or a loser. The bully is merely deflecting their own hurt feelings.

The person being bullied needs to know they do not deserve to be mistreated or abused by anyone for any reason. Stand tall. Square your shoulders and take back what is rightfully yours: your dignity, your self-esteem, your self-worth and your life.

may, you

may you find happiness

may you find love

may your heart never grow weary

may you no longer get shoved

may you find courage when times are tough

may you never lose strength

may you never give up

may you stay the course

may you never lose sight

may you admit when you are wrong

may you rejoice when you are right

may you come to realize you have so much to give

may you know here and now the time has come to live.

breaking news for bullies: freedom of speech does not include the right to mouth-off hate-fueled speech and be a deliberate jerk to someone just because you have issues of your own and need someone to take them out on.

what is positive?

hope

amazing

capable

wise

confident

strong

love

talented

over-comer

happy

optimistic

reassure

praise

amazing

to be honest

#tbh

good days 80%

bad days 20%

#tbh

The #tbh *(to be honest),* section of the book is not about pep talking you into a better mood by seeing the silver lining of a dark cloud or cuddling kittens and puppies while standing underneath a rainbow.

The phrase, *"Everything is going to be perfect from now on",* is a lie. It won't. Everyone's life has ups and downs. Things will get better, but they will never be perfect. Once again, perfection is an unrealistic, unattainable expectation.

Even though you may deal with more garbage than others, have faith in yourself that you can handle whatever life throws your way. Even if your faith is the size of a mustard seed. A small amount of faith still counts.

The truth you hopefully learned about your bullying situation from the prior pages of this book, should help you begin to make positive changes in your life and adjust your negative thought process.

Positive changes are what you need to focus your time and attention on. Starting now. You have wasted enough time being bullied.

Some of what you are about to read might sound familiar. But sometimes good points bear repeating. But, I promise you, there will be no judgements, criticisms, bashing or bullsh**ing. Only the truth.

Change is a good thing. People tend to buck change due to the discomfort or a fear of the unknown. Yes, change can suck sometimes, too. But, like it or not, life is about change. Nothing ever stays the same. So, either roll with it or get run over. Your choice.

What you have the power to change is how you look at things. The choice has always been yours. Maybe you did not realize it until just now.

You can choose to look at your life as hopeless and negative. You can choose to throw out that old way of thinking and start over. Or, you can do nothing.

No one can get inside of your head and turn your thinking process around. Only you have the power to make that happen. You have a choice to make.

Don't you think it is time to take control of your life?

#tbh:

Stop allowing negative people to speak negative words into your life. Stop believing negative things being spoken about you. If you easily believe the negative things, you can just as easily believe the positive things, too.

Get out a piece of paper and draw three columns.

in the first column:
Write down the negative things you think/feel about yourself.

in the second column:
Write down the negative things a bully(s) says about you.

in the third column:
Write down the positive things you think/feel about yourself.

Now look at it. Columns 1 and 2 are longer than column 3, right? But, guess what? The first 2 columns are garbage. Tear up Columns 1 and 2.

Take column 3 and put it up on your bedroom wall or inside your locker. Anytime you start believing the negative words from Columns 1 and 2, put your focus on Column 3.

You might be thinking, *"I don't think anything good about myself."* Everyone may have a million things they hate about themselves, but somewhere down inside hides one good thing they like about themselves. Take some time and really think about what you do like about yourself.

The truth: sometimes it is hard to override the negative and focus on the positive. But, it can be done with determination and choice.

#tbh:

Do you remember the section in the book about how much time you have wasted focusing on the bully and the effects of their negativity in your life?

Do not tear yourself down over it. Focus on the positive. Forget about the negative. Again, with determination and choice, bullying can be overcome.

#tbh:

Self-acceptance is important. It is more important than having acceptance or approval from others. If you cannot love and accept yourself, how do you expect anyone to do the same? So, love yourself, even if others never do.

#tbh:

Do not commit suicide because of bullying. Bullies are not worth it. You are worth something. Ignore what they say to you. Choose to live.

#tbh:

You are special.
You are important.
You are wonderful.
You are beautiful inside and out.
You are smart.
You are talented.
You are gifted.
You are unique.
You are important.
You just are.

DREAM

#tbh:

You deal. You heal.

#tbh:

You take control of the pain from being bullied instead of the pain taking control of you.

#tbh:

Time is a great healer. Give yourself time and you will.

FAITH

#tbh:

Today will be different than yesterday. Tomorrow might be even better. Yesterday is over. Let it go.

#tbh:

The sun always rises the next day bringing with it a chance to start over.

HOPE

#tbh:

You are not a problem. You have a problem. A bully. And, problems can always be resolved.

#tbh:

Start seeing your future through the eyes of '*can do*' instead of the eyes of '*can't do*'.

#tbh:

Sometimes a chat with a trusted adult like your parents, a teacher, a pastor, a counselor or a bully prevention hotline can help if you are being bullied. There is nothing wrong with asking for help.

LOVE

#tbh:

A bully is emotionally and mentally dysfunctional. They inflict pain upon others, hoping to feel better about themselves.

Did you know, a bully's own self-hate could rival the misery you feel about yourself? It's true.

Like you, a bully has choices. They can choose to change their behavior or remain in a life of misery. It is their choice and bears no reflection on you or anything you say or do. The problem is them. Not you.

Bullying someone is not cool. It only reveals how broken they are inside.

#tbh:

Sometimes a bully can indirectly bring something to your attention you have been carrying around inside, like a painful memory, but you never realized it before.

#tbh:

Are you ready to get to the root of your pain and heal?

TALENTED

#tbh:

Ending your life
Brings sweet relief
But leaves behind loved ones
Tormented and full of grief

The bully is the only one
Filled to the brim with joy
Mocking you even after death
Gloating over whom they destroyed.

Suicide is not the answer to your problem(s).

#tbh:

You are okay, Kid!

#tbh:

All of life is precious whether it is something as small as a beetle or someone as imperfectly made as you. *"Imperfectly"* because no one is perfect.

Striving to be perfect is a waste of time. It is an unachievable and unrealistic goal meant to steal the joy out of your life.

#tbh:

To heal from the pain caused by a bully or anyone who harmed you, you need to forgive them.

"What? Why should I do that? They hurt me."

Because forgiving someone who has hurt you is how you let go of the pain and heal. It does not mean you must be friends with them, tell them you forgive them or forget what they did to you.

Even after you have forgiven someone who did you wrong, it might not feel that way. This is a normal feeling. You need time for the initial hatred to fade.

"Why should I forgive someone who did me so wrong?"

You do it for your own self-preservation. You do it because it is the right thing to do. You do it because it is healthier, mentally and physically, to walk in love instead of bitterness and hate.

Forgiveness is something you must realize within yourself. Forgiveness must be something you are willing to do from the heart. Nobody can make you forgive someone. Only you have the power to make that choice.

You may not feel like forgiving someone who has been unbelievably cruel to you. But, you should consider giving it a try. Not for their sake. For yours.

Back in the old days, when someone committed a murder against another, the Romans would tie the corpse to the murderer. As the body rotted, the murderer became sick with disease and died a miserable death.

It is a proven fact that anger and the unwillingness to forgive will make you sick. Is a bully worth doing that to your health?

#tbh:

Any amount of gratitude, whether the size of a mustard seed or as large as a boulder, can give you a better attitude about life. It is not easy to hold the line and remain positive when things are going wrong. But, with determination and effort it can be managed. Things will go your way if you believe they can. It's the power of positive thinking. It works.

ACCOMPLISHED

#tbh:

See yourself as worthy: worthy of having good friends, a joyful life, being treated with dignity and respect. If you do not see yourself as worthy or recognize your value, how do you expect others to? Believe you are worthy, and soon others will, too.

#tbh:

Have you been making personal sacrifices to please someone else while destroying your own life in the process? Are you making these sacrifices to seek someone's approval?

Ask yourself these two questions:

"Why do I need their approval?"
"Why does their opinion of me matter so much?"

You should never sacrifice who you are as a person to please someone else. Respect is earned, not bought. Respect yourself. Stand up for yourself and what you believe in, no matter what anyone else thinks. Just don't be a jerk about it.

#tbh:

Retrain your brain to *"I can"* not *"I can't"*.

VALUABLE

#tbh:

Words always matter. Words can lift you up. Words can tear you down. Always choose them wisely.

#tbh:

If you are failing school because of being bullied, there are two things you need to do: stop focusing on the bully and get focused on yourself.

Bullying is ruining your future. It needs to stop right now. Try setting a goal for yourself to start bringing your grades back up before the school year ends. Make it a realistic goal. The object is to help you, not stress you out. For example: go up one grade or even half of a grade - like a C to a C+.

When negativity strikes, it is very important you remain focused on the positive things in your life.

It is pointless to destroy your future over someone who (believe it or not) will not even matter a year from now. Do not give a bully the power to wreck your future.

#tbh:

Staying true to yourself is the best thing in the world you can do.

CAPABLE

#tbh:

You have the right to feel good about yourself, even if someone does not agree you should.

#tbh:

Everyone has the potential to be *something* and to be *somebody.*

Being somebody does not mean being famous. Being somebody can be as simple as: being a person who is kind to others or a person who sets goals and tries to accomplish things in life.

You are somebody with the power and ability to be anything and everything you want to be. Never quit, compromise or give up on yourself.

AMAZING

#tbh:

Contrary to what you might think about yourself or what others may have told you, you are not weak. You are not a loser. You are not pathetic. You are not a slut. You are not a nerd, a dork or a geek. Why are you giving negativity a place in your life and ignoring the positive stuff? Did you know you can choose to put the bullying garbage out on the curb and stop tolerating it in your life?

#tbh:

Boundaries are meant to protect you. They help you maintain control of your life. Boundaries are not about becoming a diva or a snob. The purpose of setting boundaries is to not allow people to abuse you physically, mentally or emotionally. Setting boundaries will ensure you are to be treated with respect, dignity and courtesy or not at all. What boundaries are you prepared to set?

#tbh:

Respect yourself enough to never settle for anything less than what you would do to or for another.

#tbh:

Did you know you have a right to protect yourself?
Did you know you do not have to tolerate abuse?
Did you know you can speak up and ask for help?

Being mistreated by someone is unacceptable behavior on their part. You should never allow someone to have that kind of abusive power over you.

DARING

#tbh:

Did you know everyone is going through stuff?

Granted, their issues may or may not be as serious as yours. But, to them, they are the most important thing in the world. You are not the only one in pain, feeling hurt, disappointment, sorrow, anger, confusion, sadness or depression.

Everyone, from your teacher, to your parents, to your friends, are all dealing with something - including your bully. Though it may appear everything is perfect in their life, do not be fooled. Some people are good at hiding their issues or handling them better than others.

You are not alone in having to *"deal with stuff"*. Everyone must deal with unpleasant issues at some point. Nobody rides for free in the ups and downs of life.

"Okay. But, how does this help me when it comes to being bullied?"

You need to understand that the bully has issues they are dealing with, too.

"Yeah, but the stuff I am dealing with is because of the bully. What about that?"

The difference between you and a bully is: they choose to act out their pain by behaving like a jerk. And you choose to react when they do.

"How else am I supposed to act when someone hurts my feelings?"

The natural reaction is pain. But, although you may feel it, you do not have to act on it and show a bully they got to you. Think about it.

A bully strikes out at someone to help ease the pain they are dealing with down inside. For them to stop feeling pain for even a second, they must take it out on someone. It is inexcusable, unacceptable, thoughtless, abusive behavior on their part.

But they are choosing to behave that way. You can choose not to react to it from now on. Just because someone dishes garbage to you does not mean you must accept it.

#tbh:

You have nothing to prove to anyone other than yourself.

#tbh:

If you want to feel whole and complete, first, love yourself.

#tbh:

Those who love you for you will be there. Those who want to use you, show them the door.

HONEST

#tbh:

You can flee from a bully, but you cannot escape from yourself. Acknowledge your issues and pain. Then, heal from it and move on.

#tbh:

Looking up to or imitating someone who lacks patience, kindness, a tolerance for others, acts prideful, rude, nasty, violent, or spreads hurtful gossip, is physically abusive, lies, yells, cusses people out, is not a good example on how to behave and be respected by others.

#tbh:

Always be polite until there is a valid reason for you not to be. Treat others how you would like to be treated, even if they fail to return the same. You do it not to win their approval or because you expect something in return. You do it because it is the right way to behave.

#tbh:

Take the high road, when someone takes the low road with you. It is not always easy to walk in love when someone is so hateful towards you, but you will be a better person for having done so.

KIND

#tbh:

Love grows and flourishes. Hate withers and dies at the root. Better to love than hate.

#tbh:

There is a saying out there that goes something like this:
"The dash between your date of birth and the date of your death is your life."

Make your dash count.
Your life matters.
You matter.
Never forget that.

#tbh:

Always do your best. If it is not good enough for someone, they are not good enough for you.

#tbh:

Learning to love yourself, after years of self-hatred, takes time. Be patient with yourself.

#tbh:

If somebody loves and respects you, they will not force you to send naked pictures of yourself to them.

note: *Check your State Law. If sexted pictures you received are from someone under the age of eighteen, you are in possession of child pornography. You could face criminal charges, jail time and must register as a sex offender.*

No matter how much in love you might be or how great you think the person you are with is, you need to know that feelings change. The same person you thought would never hurt you, could destroy you. Protect yourself. If someone walks out of your life because you would not send them naked pictures of yourself, then they did not care about you from the beginning. They were only using you. You deserve better.

THANKFUL

#tbh:

So, you have a problem with a bully. But, you are afraid to tell someone about it. You fear that if you talk to an adult, you will be made fun of or seen as being weak or uncool. Or, you are afraid your problem might be viewed as unimportant or silly when it feels like a matter of life or death to you.

You should not have to wake up every day feeling sad, depressed or angry over someone's thoughtless actions towards you. If that is how you are feeling, you need to talk to someone you trust about it. And, by someone, I mean preferably an adult. Yes, you can talk to your friends, but they might not know what to do or they could violate your trust and blab it around school.

Knowledge is power. You acknowledge that you have a problem and need help for that problem. This is a powerful step towards healing. Do you realize that? Find someone you feel comfortable enough talking to and share what is bugging you. Once you start talking about it, you will feel like a giant weight is lifted off you.

#tbh:

The phrase, *"It's hopeless"* is a lie. Life is full of challenges. Some you will win. Some you will lose. Nobody can be a success all the time. It's unrealistic. The key is to remain balanced when changes and challenges arise.

#tbh:

No situation is ever hopeless. You may feel like right now you have no control over your life, but that is not true. You DO have control. You have had control all along. You just did not realize it until now.

#tbh:

You have a good future ahead of you, even if it does not look like it right now.

GENUINE

#tbh:

The mind is a powerful thing. It can make you see the good. It can also make you see the bad. It can influence you to do right. It can influence you to do wrong. It can make you believe lies and rumors a bully spread about you. It can also make you believe positive things people say about you. It is all in what you allow to come into your head and take root inside your heart. Although the mind is a powerful thing, you are still the one who is in control. You are the one who has the power to choose what you want to believe.

#tbh:

Stop comparing yourself to others. You are beautifully and wonderfully made. You are perfectly flawed, as you should be. You are not perfect. You never will be. Neither will anyone else. Those unique qualities you get picked on for, are what make you special. There is no one else like you on the planet. Be proud of who you are and never allow anyone to make you feel bad about yourself.

#tbh:

Put your right hand on your left shoulder, your left hand on your right shoulder. Now give yourself a hug.

#tbh:

Please, aspire to love yourself. Not with arrogance or pride. Love yourself with appreciation, joy and kindness. Take the time to get to know who you are as an individual. I have said it before, but it bears repeating. For others to love and accept you, you must first love yourself. If you do not love yourself, how do you expect anyone else to love you? There are plenty of reasons to love yourself. Just look in the mirror.

FAB

#tbh:

Never feel ashamed or bad about yourself if you fail. Part of trying anything is failing. It is okay to fail. You tried. And that counts for something. So, what if you fail? Big deal. People try and fail all the time. If you happen to fail at something, try again until you succeed. Failure is viewed as a bad thing only if you never tried in the first place.

#tbh:

Believe in yourself.

#tbh:

You do not have to play the hand you were dealt. The beauty of cards is you can always change them or reshuffle the deck.

HAPPY

#tbh:

God does not make mistakes. You are not a mistake. You are not a disgrace. You are not a screw-up. You are not worthless. You are not naïve. You are not a loser. But, you are not perfect, either. No one is. You are going to be okay.

#tbh:

Do not grow weak and weary during trying times. Those who persevere stand strong like a tree against a mighty wind. Those who are weak snap like a twig in a light breeze. Things will get better. They have too. Do not give up. You are a strong mighty tree.

#tbh:

Nothing is ever hopeless or out of reach. Nothing is ever an overnight fix, either. If it were, we would all be going around twitching our noses like Samantha from the TV Show *"Bewitched"*. But that is not real life. Real life is ups and downs. Everything takes work. That is the truth.

MOTIVATED

#tbh:

You have nothing to be sorry for.

#tbh:

Do ever wish you were someone other than you?

Stop thinking this way.

The only person you need to be is yourself. There is nothing wrong with you. If you think there is, that is a choice you are choosing to make based on false ideas you have of yourself or what a bully has said to you. You can choose to accept yourself, just as easily as you can reject yourself.

You should know not everything is as it seems. People are good at hiding shameful secrets and pain. Stop putting yourself down and comparing yourself to others. You do not know what goes on behind closed doors in their life.

If you do not like something about yourself then change it. But, change it for you. Do not make any changes to yourself or your life because you are trying to please someone else. Being a people-pleaser is a waste of your time.

VICTORIOUS

#tbh:

Establish a healthy relationship with yourself. It does not have to be perfect. No relationship ever is. All relationships take effort and commitment.

#tbh:

It is a good thing sometimes to spend some *"me time"* getting to know who you are. Get to know who you are as a spirit and a soul. Only you can know who you truly are down inside. Do not be afraid to get to know yourself. Stepping outside of our comfort zone and learning who we are is a good thing. It can be an exciting time to learn what you like and who you want to be in life.

#tbh:

Exit the pothole ridden road which you have been traveling down. It is time to hit the metaphoric *"open road"*, roll the windows down and enjoy a new journey.

#tbh:

You are not worthless.

#tbh:

If you take the high road you will not get a nose bleed. Sometimes the best way to handle someone who has done you wrong is to do nothing. If they cannot upset you, the thrill for them is gone. You win - they lose. Pretty neat trick, huh?

STRONG

#tbh:

Stop living in the past. You cannot undue what has been done. It is finished. It is pointless to continue dipping back into the *"what was"* or *"what could have been"* or *"how it should be"*. Let it go. Live in the present. It is time to take a bold step towards a future that can be anything you choose it to be. You are in control of it.

#tbh:

There will never be another you. Appreciate your life. Take care of yourself. Love yourself.

OPTIMISTIC

#tbh:

You have a mind. The bully does not matter.

#tbh:

Recognizing the root cause of an issue gets you 50% closer to resolving it and living a more peaceful life.

SERENE

#tbh:

Beware of the metaphoric octopus tentacle that brings about past hurts and other negative stuff in your life.

There will always be a tentacle from the past trying to ensnare you and keep you from moving forward. The tentacle is meant to make you feel your situation is never going to change or getting better. It is a lie and a deception.

When a tentacle from the past tries to enter your mind or your life, say, *"Be gone!"* and then continue moving forward.

You have the choice not to be trapped in misery due to lies, deception and situations that have long been over. While you cannot undo what has already been done, you can choose to not let it hinder you anymore. Severe the tentacles from the past. Be free.

#tbh:

Ask yourself this one important question:
"Who am I?"
Not,
"Who am I according to what others think of me?"

Get a journal and write down everything about yourself from your likes to dislikes, favorite things, stuff you cannot stand, what you love about yourself, what you wish you could change about yourself and why, etc... Find out who you are for you, not who you are according to how others define you.

#tbh:

The beautiful thing about life is you get to start over again and again, no matter how many times you mess up. The same cannot be said about death. Death is final.

INSIGHTFUL

#tbh:

Even if you are being treated like a social outcast, try and be a friend to someone who you think may be in the same boat. Taking your mind off your own troubles and giving time to another does wonders for your self-esteem. You never know what type of impact your gesture of kindness could have on someone in pain. It might literally be their last life line.

#tbh:

These five words can mean a lot to someone in pain: *"I am here. I care."*

#tbh:

The only person you must please when you look in the mirror is yourself.

#tbh:

The only two places the word *"Perfect"* exists is in a dictionary and the Bible. Stop exhausting yourself trying to be someone you cannot possibly ever be. Perfect.

#tbh:

Forgive those who have done you wrong. Forgive yourself for things you said or did or allowed to happen. Forgiveness is the key to releasing the hurt and healing.

YOUTHFUL

#tbh:

Not being popular or not having alot of friends should never make you feel bad about yourself. This is no reflection on you as a person. Having a few friends, one friend or even no friends does not make you any less of a person than someone who does.

"School Popularity" is a brief time in your life, not your entire life. You should never look at not being popular as *"the end of the world"*. So, what if you don't become prom queen, head cheerleader, school stud or the class president? It is okay if you want to strive for those titles, but if you do not achieve them, know you are still a terrific person.

#tbh:

What matters is quality, not quantity, in every area of your life.

BLESSED

#tbh:

Sometimes life stinks. But, that's no reason to quit living it.

#tbh:

Things will work out.

WISE

#tbh:

Laughter really is the best medicine when you are feeling down. Laughing releases feel good hormones called endorphins which make you happy. Try laughing. It might help make you feel better, even if only for a little while.

#tbh:

When you have done all you can do, stand tall.

DETERMINED

#tbh:

Have courage, stay committed, remain consistent and you can achieve anything in life.

#tbh:

You are the head and not the tail! You are above and not beneath! Never forget it!

#tbh:

Even though things may appear bleak and you feel like you have wasted your time or missed out on things, know that you have not. Everything you think you have been robbed of will come into your life even better than you could have ever imagined. If you stay focused on getting your life in order, things will work out for your benefit.

EXCEPTIONAL

#tbh:

You were born for a good purpose in life. Your Creator knew you even before you were born. And, even though right now, you might be feeling like your purpose is to be treated like garbage, please know that is simply not true.

You are loved. God loves you. People in your life love you even if they have a tough time saying it or showing you. You are not alone. You really aren't. There is nothing that will stop God from loving you and wanting only the best for your life. God is love. He loves you unconditionally. Love yourself, too. You are worthy of being loved. You deserve to be loved.

#tbh:

Imperfections are beautiful.

#tbh:

Be in the present. Let go of the past. Look forward to your future.

OVERCOMER

the end of the book.

the beginning of your new life.

q & a

normandy d. piccolo

questions & answers

normandy d. piccolo

Q. How did you become involved with bullying?
I was severely bullied from the age of five until my mid-twenties.

Q. Were you ever suicidal because of being bullied?
Yes. It did reach a point where I attempted suicide one time.

Q. What stopped you from ending your life?
I realized that if I ended my life, the bullies won. And, they were not worth my life. I decided I wanted to no longer be a victim. I wanted to overcome the pain and help bullied kids to not feel the horrific pain I had experienced for years.

Q. Did you write 'Bullied Dying to Fit In' as a way to help you heal from being bullied? It is put together in an unusual format, not like most books about bullying.
Yes and no. Yes, because it did help me heal as the words poured forth.

But the main reason I chose to write *'Bullied Dying to Fit In'* and, in that particular format, was because the market is flooded with so many "my bully story" books. I wanted the reader to know that "I get it". I understand how they feel because I have been there. But, at the same time, I also wanted to allow the reader *(a person who is being bullied)* to see it as "their story". I also wrote it this way for those who have never been bullied, to help them realize how painful it is to be bullied. And, I am hoping to help parents who have a child being bullied or lost a child who was bullied to understand the pain and maybe answer some of the 'whys' which are often asked after a tragedy.

Q. What do you hope the book accomplishes for those who are being bullied?
By the turn of the last page, I want bullied kids to see their future in a positive light and to heal from the pain and know that they are not alone. The

book contains five sections; hurting, facts, scoop, healing and #tbh, which range from the pain of being bullied, to information, to the bold truth about bullying and how to gain strength to rise above it.

Q. How do we end bullying?
Unfortunately, there will always be bullying. Bullying exists even in the animal and insect world. As for humans, hopefully through better education programs at school, more communication at home with their parents, the teaching of basic manners, learning how to agree to disagree and develop better acceptance and tolerance of others. As a society we need to become more sensitized and less desensitized. This happens by having more human contact vs electronic communication. Taking these steps, a bullied victim will better understand how to stop being a victim and see their bully through new eyes. The same goes for the bully. Hopefully he or she will learn how to better communicate with others without using physical, mental or emotional abuse towards them.

Q. What was one of the most surprising things you learned while writing 'Bullied Dying to Fit In'?
I discovered I had a lot of pain that was tucked away down inside that I never dealt with.

Q. And have you since dealt with the pain?
I have. But, I would be lying if I told you everything in my life is perfect since dealing with and healing from the pain. Perfection is an unrealistic goal. And, if anyone tells you otherwise, they are mistaken.

Q. If you had one piece of advice to give, what would it be?
Life throws us challenges every day. It's how we choose to handle those challenges that makes us or breaks us. You have the power – you have had it all along. The power of choice. You can choose to allow a bully to ruin your life. Or, you can choose to take your life back. Your choice.

Q. What do you think makes a good story?
The truth.

Q. What were your goals and intentions in this book?
To help someone not feel the way I did about myself for the longest time because of bullying. Having people hate you hurts. And, I did hate myself right along with the bullies. When someone says hateful things about you over and over, it's hard not to believe them after a while.

Q. How do you feel you achieved your goals and intentions in 'Bullied Dying to Fit In'?
If I help only one person overcome bullying and heal, then mission accomplished.

Q. What was the hardest part of writing this book?
I would have to say the section entitled, "hurting" because I had to reach deep down inside and basically bear mine and every bullied person's soul. It was a very painful, and yet at the same time healing journey. Being bullied is very damaging to a person mentally, physically and emotionally. It goes deeper than I think most people realize.

Q. What did you enjoy most about writing this book?
I really enjoyed writing the section entitled, "#tbh" because it is truthful, honest and positive. The section talks to you, not at you. So, for those who have no one to talk to or get advice from, this section can be helpful.

Also, by Normandy D. Piccolo

Why is Kristyn A. Kutter?

Why is Kristyn A. Kutter? won two awards and was placed in the TOP 10 List for Fiction/Non-Fiction and the Fiction Recommendation List.

2021 In the Margins Book Award/ School Library Journal

You may know my name, but not my life story. To be honest, it's rather cliché for a girl of seventeen and three-quarters. But it's far from boring. Self-loathing. Depression. Loneliness. Liar-liar pants on fire. Secretive. Rebellious. *Blah-blah-blah-blah.* You get the idea.

I feel absolutely nothing until a razor blade touches my skin. I'm known to do other crazy things to myself out of pure spite. Yeah, I hate myself that much. I'll take hits of MDMA and dance until dawn trying to forget. Other times, I'll randomly hookup with total wankers when my self-esteem lands in the loo. Which is pretty much all the time, lately. Bugger!

My best mate, Maddison, killed herself. Bitch! I guess she couldn't handle life. Staring down at the random cuts on my body, I can't say I'm doing that much better. But, end up in a red mahogany casket with white velvet interior, like Maddison? I'm not sure.

Maddison's death, Jamey *(my ex and an absolute tosser)* and teen drama from Claire and the *Posh Miss Perfects* have forced me to make a choice. Deal with my issues or keep repeating the same self-destructive behavior over and again, expecting a different result.

You may have heard what I've done, but not what I've been through or where I'm going.

You're 'bout to find out.

***Trigger Warning:** Includes strong language, non-graphic depictions of self-harm, drug and alcohol usage and sexual situations. Recommended for ages 16+*.

Why is Kristyn A. Kutter? discusses serious and difficult issues regarding self-harm, depression and suicide. If you or anyone you know are struggling with any of those issues, please seek help at a support or crisis center in your area or online through local and national organizations.

National Alliance on Mental Illness (NAMI)
800-950-6264(NAMI)
info@nami.org
Text "NAMI" to 741741

Suicide Prevention Lifeline
800-273-8255

SELF-HARM IS NEVER THE ANSWER.
SUICIDE IS NEVER THE ANSWER.

www.ingramcontent.com/pod-product-compliance
Lightning Source LLC
Chambersburg PA
CBHW071951040426
42447CB00009B/1305
* 9 7 8 0 9 9 7 9 3 4 9 4 6 *